HOW TO
BUILD A FENCE

Plan and Build Basic Fences and Gates

—

Jeff Beneke

T0385243

Storey Publishing

The mission of Storey Publishing is to serve our customers by publishing practical information that encourages personal independence in harmony with the environment.

Edited by Carleen Madigan and Philip Schmidt
Series design by Alethea Morrison
Art direction by Jeff Stiefel
Text production by Theresa Wiscovitch
Indexed by Christine Lindemer, Boston Road Communications

Cover illustration by © Steve Sanford
Interior illustrations by Melanie Powell

Portions of this text were originally published in *The Fence Bible* by Jeff Beneke (Storey Publishing, 2005).

Storey books are available for special premium and promotional uses and for customized editions. For further information, please call 1-800-793-9396.

Storey Publishing
210 MASS MoCA Way
North Adams, MA 01247
www.storey.com

Printed in the United States by McNaughton & Gunn, Inc.
10 9 8 7 6 5 4 3 2 1

LIBRARY OF CONGRESS CATALOGING-IN-PUBLICATION DATA

Beneke, Jeff.
  How to build a fence : plan and build basic fences and gates / by Jeff Beneke.
    pages cm. — (A Storey basics title)
  Includes index.
  ISBN 978-1-61212-442-1 (pbk. : alk. paper)
  ISBN 978-1-61212-443-8 (ebook) 1. Fences—Design and construction—Amateurs' manuals. 2. Gates—Design and construction—Amateurs' manuals. I. Title.
TH4965.B46 2015
690'.89—dc23
                          2014033712

CONTENTS

For Molly, Erica, and Kathryn.
My inspiration. My hopes. My heroes.

INTRODUCTION

The 3-foot-high grape-stake fencing that lines my property is showing its age. On one side, the fence has been overwhelmed by a neighbor's newer, higher, and more solid privacy fence.

In back, the same fencing separates our yard from an apple orchard. The small gate has completely fallen over, and deer, raccoons, humans, and other creatures pass through without a thought.

My fence, in other words, might easily be viewed as a very poor example of the type of fencing this book seeks to help you design, build, and maintain. It is largely useless and mostly overlooked and can barely stand on its own any more. You, to the contrary, want a fence that serves a vital function, looks great, and can be expected to be standing strong years from now.

That, at any rate, is one way of looking at it. Here's another: I like my fence. It, like my house, is nearing 70 years of age, and, also like the house, it was built with a high level of quality and integrity. The hundreds of hand-split redwood stakes that define the fence are, for the most part, still solid and free of rot.

The wood's well-earned patina — wrinkles, pockmarks, and all — exudes the sense of pride that living a long, healthy life commands. Once I've finished remodeling the interior of the house, I'll turn my attention to that old fence. I'll remove parts of it and reuse some of the stakes for garden fencing.

And if I decide I really have no use for the rest of the other stakes, I'll sell them. Good quality grape stakes are much in demand here in California wine country. My old fence embodies the essence of sustainable building practices — no landfills required. The next time I build a new fence, it's a lesson that will drive my design.

CHAPTER ONE

PLANNING, DESIGN, AND LAYOUT

The planning and design phase of fence building involves much more than choosing a style, materials, and decorative elements. There are laws to satisfy (not to mention neighbors and homeowner association boards), as well as numerous design considerations, both practical and aesthetic. Many of your decisions will hinge on your answers to two big questions: 1) Why are you building the fence? and 2) How will the fence affect the look, the function, and the feel of your home and landscape? When you're ready to take your ideas from the drawing board to the ground, a few simple layout techniques will help you get it right.

FENCE LAW

FENCES OFTEN ARE SUBJECT TO strict legal definitions and restrictions. Building codes, zoning ordinances, and homeowners associations may specify whether or not you can build a fence at all, what style of fence you can build, how high the fence can be, and how far it must be kept from a property line or street.

Start your research at your local building department, typically an office of city government. Many city websites include checklists that outline the basic rules and restrictions for fences, as well as what types of projects need permits. In addition, it's also a good idea to talk with a department official to confirm that your fence plan meets all requirements — even if you're confident you won't need a permit. Be prepared to explain the fence in detail and where you want to build it (how close to the neighbors' property, sidewalks, streets, and so forth). Your local building code may have minimal requirements other than those mentioned in this book.

You should also make preparations to have your property marked for underground electrical, plumbing, and other service lines. (See Before You Start Digging on page 29.)

Building Permits and Zoning Restrictions

If your fence project needs a building permit, your local building department will provide you with details for obtaining one. Be sure to find out what information you need to submit to the building department, how much the permit will cost, how long you are likely to have to wait to get it, and at what stage or stages you will need to have the fence inspected. If you plan to take your time building the fence, you should also ask how long the permit will remain valid; most permits are valid for no more than 1 year.

Most zoning laws relate to property lines and property use, both of which can affect your fence design. Common restrictions include a 3-foot height limit on fences facing the street and a 6-foot limit on side and backyard fences. Another restriction is the setback. Often, you can't build a fence right up to the edge of your property line. Instead, you must set it back several feet from the line.

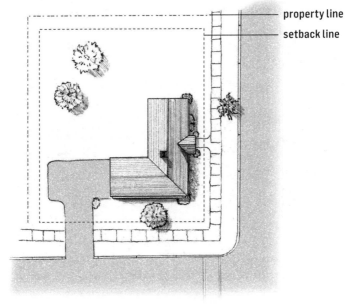

property line

setback line

A MINOR SETBACK. Even though you own the property out to the property line, you may not be allowed to add new construction beyond the setback line.

When a Fence Is Not a Fence

If you run into a code or zoning problem with a fence project, it's worthwhile finding out exactly what the relevant board considers to be a "fence." You may find that a fence is defined as something that is built, and not something that is planted. If you are prohibited from building a fence high enough to suit your needs, you may still be allowed to plant a hedgerow or some trees that can meet the height you need. Such a "living fence" offers little security and won't corral animals, but it can be an effective privacy screen. And neighbors might be much less offended by some shrubbery than by a solid fence. Hedgerows can be created with trimmed shrubs, ornamental grasses, small evergreen trees, even living bamboo.

Another potential solution for building a fence higher than allowed is to offer to use a more transparent material, such as metal or lattice, on top of the solid lower portion of fencing.

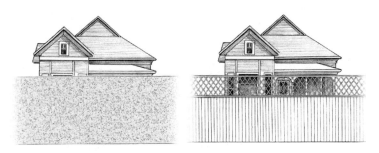

A HIGH, SOLID FENCE OR WALL (left) may not be allowed by local code, but you might be able to achieve the same effect by building a shorter fence and topping it with lattice (right) or vines.

VARIANCES

If you want to build a fence 20 feet from the street, but a zoning law says it must be at least 30 feet away, you can apply for a variance (special permission to build something that violates existing requirements). Don't hesitate to apply for one if you feel you have a legitimate argument, and be prepared to do some research and present a good case.

Take the time to understand the law and learn why your fence might not follow it. If the issue is public safety, such as with fences on corner lots restricting traffic visibility, you probably won't win your case. On the other hand, if you want to build a privacy fence to block an unpleasant view but the view is uphill from the fence location, you might be able to successfully argue that a height limit of 6 feet is too restrictive for your needs.

Easements

An easement defines the rights of parties other than the property owner to use the property for specific purposes. For example, utility companies may have a right to drive their trucks through your property to tend to repairs. Shared driveway arrangements between adjoining properties are other protected areas.

Easements typically are noted in title reports (ask your title insurance company for a copy if you don't have one), and it's the homeowner's obligation to know about them. A fence that violates an easement may have to be taken down at the owner's expense. If you have any concerns about easements, it might be wise to discuss the matter with a real estate attorney.

FENCING WITH A PURPOSE

EVERY MAJOR DECISION ABOUT fence design is best made with specific goals in mind. Often, various needs and functions overlap, which means you'll likely have to prioritize and prepare for compromises. For example, if security is your sole objective, you might choose a type of fence that has little visual appeal. But if you also want your fence to be an attractive addition to your property, you may have to sacrifice a bit of security in favor of a nicer looking fence.

Privacy and Security

The two goals of privacy and security often go together in fence design, but not always. Privacy fences can substantially expand the usable living space of your house, turning much

....

Marking (and Decorating) Boundaries

Boundary fences offer simple comfort, neither blocking views nor discouraging conversations. They define limits without excluding. Typically low and simple, a boundary fence subtly reminds neighborhood athletes that your front yard is not a soccer field, just as it encourages visitors to approach the house via the sidewalk. Many boundary fences are built simply for visual impact, perhaps to break the monotony of a large stretch of turf or to provide a backdrop for a garden or a support for climbing vines. Classic choices for boundaries include picket, post-and-rail, and ornamental metal fences.

....

of your yard into functional outdoor rooms where you can sit, read, relax, and converse without feeling that you are on display. A good fence designer will think about privacy fences the way an interior decorator might think about walls, and try to create different colors and textures to help define different "outdoor rooms."

Privacy is usually achieved by way of a high fence with solid or near-solid infill — the slats, planks, or other materials that make up the fence panels. Board fences are the most common choice, but a thick row of hedges could also achieve the same end result.

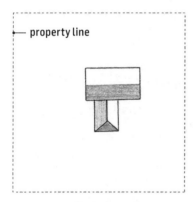

small privacy realm

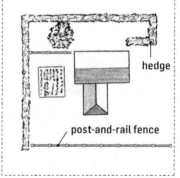

large privacy realm

IN A PROPERTY WITH AN OPEN EXPANSE OF YARD (left), privacy is confined to the house interior. Fences effectively enlarge the living space by expanding the privacy realm away from the house (right).

By contrast, a security fence is designed to discourage intruders from going over, under, or, in extreme cases, through the structure. Height and sharp edges can address the first concern, while strength and ground-hugging construction can handle the second. Chain-link fences are easy to install and relatively inexpensive (if unattractive) options for security. A wood fence is hard to kick through but easy to saw through. For combining good looks and solid security without blocking views, a fence made with ornamental metal is tough to beat.

Gate construction is frequently the weak link in a security fence. The hinges must be strong and fastened securely to both the gate and the post, and the latch should be lockable and jimmy-proof.

Controlling the Elements

Wind, snow, and noise can all be subdued with the right type of fence in the right place.

Fences for shade. Like shade trees that prevent the summer sun from heating up a house, a fence can shade a driveway, sidewalk, or patio to reduce heat buildup in the solid mass. It can also shade the side of the house from early morning and late evening sun.

Fences for windbreaks. In cold climates, wind contributes to heat loss. A fence can reduce the velocity of the wind striking your house and thus potentially reduce heating bills. Contrary to what you might think, a solid fence typically isn't the best windbreak. It's better to let some wind pass through, such as with horizontal louvered fence boards that are angled down toward the house. A hedgerow planted a foot or two away from a house wall can help redirect a cold breeze up and onto the roof. In warm weather, a windbreak fence can tame breezes and improve the comfort of outdoor sitting areas. *Note:* Windbreaks are effective only when placed perpendicular to the prevailing breeze, or as close to perpendicular as possible.

Fences for snow. A good windbreak fence can also control snowdrifts. Style and location are critical considerations. A solid fence creates deep drifts on both sides of the fence, while an open-style fence produces longer, shallower drifts and less snow buildup on the downwind side. Don't place a snow fence too close to a driveway or sidewalk; it should be at least as far from the passageway as the fence is high. As with windbreaks, snow fences are most effective when running perpendicular to prevailing winds.

Fences for blocking noise. Noise is airborne vibration, so a dense barrier (such as a concrete or stone wall) is the best fencing solution for reducing noise. A fence made from solid wood is the next best choice. Because fences offer minimal noise reduction, the most effective strategy for noise reduction indoors is to soundproof the house.

Pool Fencing

Swimming pools *must* be surrounded by code-approved fencing. The United States Consumer Product Safety Commission offers guidelines for safety-barrier fencing (follow the link in Resources, page 120). More importantly, check with your local building department for specific requirements in your area. Typical recommendations include (but may not be limited to):

- Ensure a minimum fence height of 48", and remove nearby objects that would facilitate climbing (garbage cans, for example).
- Avoid fence styles that are easy to climb; keep horizontal rails at least 45" apart and place them on the inside (the pool side) of the fence.
- Space pickets no more than 1¾" apart. With chain-link or lattice fencing, spaces should not exceed 1¾".
- Keep the bottom of the fence 2" to 4" aboveground to prevent crawling under.
- Include self-closing hinges and a self-latching latch on the gate. It's best to have the gate swing out, away from the pool. The latch should be set high enough so that it is out of a child's reach.

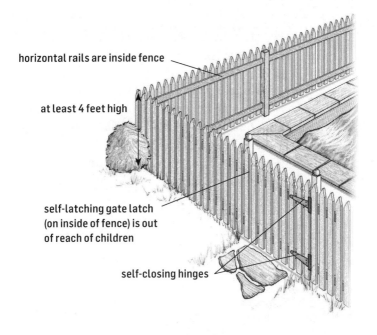

horizontal rails are inside fence

at least 4 feet high

self-latching gate latch (on inside of fence) is out of reach of children

self-closing hinges

Dog Fences

A dog fence needs to be only higher than your dog can jump. Typically, large dogs require a 6-foot-high fence and small dogs a 4-footer. If your intent is to keep other dogs out, plan on a 6-footer. Also remember that dogs can dig. Thwart a tunneling pooch by incorporating wire mesh fencing along the bottom. On the inside of the fence, extend the mesh straight down from the fence 3" to 4" into the ground, then bend the mesh and extend it horizontally about 2 feet.

STYLE AND OTHER DESIGN CONSIDERATIONS

VIEW YOUR FENCE AS an extension of your house. For inspiration, look to the trim around windows and doors. These accents could suggest decorative touches for the fence. Dominant posts on a porch may be a model for the fence posts (especially gateposts). Or you might be inspired by the house's siding or finish materials. In general, long and flat houses look good with horizontally oriented fences, while a house with a prominent gable or complex roof lines might be better complemented with a fence composed of varying heights.

THE HIGH, SOLID, and more contemporary-looking fence both obscures the house and contrasts with the house style.

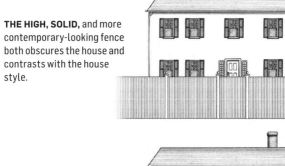

THE LOWER, MORE OPEN and more historically matching fence is a better fit.

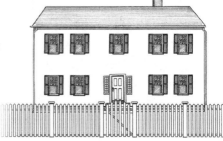

Open or Closed Style?

This question of "open or closed?" relates to the fence infill, which can range from that of a high, solid privacy fence to a low, skeletal border fence. Closed fences offer privacy but also cut off your view of the neighborhood. Open fences provide less privacy but do not block off neighborhood views. When choosing an appropriate degree of enclosure, be sure to consider the views from inside the house as well as from the yard. Open fences tend to suit front yards, while closed fences might be better suited along the sides and back of a property. (On urban lots with small yards, high and solid fences can create a buffer against noisy sidewalks and streets, and create a beneficial "out of sight, out of mind" effect.)

....

Field Research

Good designers are good observers. Take a walk or bike ride through different neighborhoods, or drive along some rural areas — camera or sketch pad in hand — with the single purpose of observing fences. You can search through magazines and conduct research online, but such activities are no substitute for looking at real fences in real yards. Don't be afraid to stop and talk to homeowners about their fences. Do-it-yourselfers are almost always more than happy to talk about their creations and to share information about their expenses, frustrations, and lessons.

....

To Gate or Not

Security and privacy fences typically require a strong, solid gate with a lock. With other fences, the inclusion of a gate is a matter of choice. Many boundary and purely decorative fences are left gateless. A gate can serve as a decorative focal point or it can blend in almost invisibly with the fence. If you choose to gate your fence, read chapter 4. During the design phase it's important to include any gates in your overall plan.

Designing with Contrasts

Contrast can be incorporated into fence design in two primary ways. The first is to differentiate the two sides of a fence. For example, with a relatively solid fence, the plain, simple face on the street side could be contrasted with a lush, decorative garden running along the fence's interior. More simply, the fence could be a light color on one side and a dark color on the other.

Incorporating differing elements is the second way to provide contrast. Consider alternating high sections with low sections, open sections with closed, hard surfaces (wood or metal) with soft (hedges or other vegetation). You can even mix materials: both wood and metal fencing pair beautifully with brick columns and gateposts.

Height and Sight

Height is most often related to the function of a fence. But height can involve additional considerations, such as legal restrictions (see Fence Law on page 4), as well as the view you wish to preserve or block, and the topography of your property.

For example, a low fence placed atop a berm or small hill can provide as much privacy as a tall fence on flat ground. Think about where you will spend much of your time when either you are outside or you are looking outside from indoors: a 6-foot fence that's close to the viewer blocks more of the view beyond than does the same fence placed farther away from the viewer. There are also technical considerations that affect the height of the fence: the taller (and heavier) the fence, the more securely it needs to be connected to the ground.

Some general rules of thumb can help you determine your fence's height:

- **The 2- to 3-foot fence.** Commonly used as a basic border around the foundation of a house or garage, perhaps to protect flower beds. Low fences can present tripping hazards and should not interrupt traffic paths.
- **The 4-foot fence.** A good height for dividing yards without dividing neighbors. Offers modest security, in general, and a fair amount of privacy for someone seated near the fence. Four feet is the recommended minimum height for safety barriers around pools and other potential dangers.
- **The 5-foot fence.** Can often be an awkward height for boundaries between properties (difficult to talk over, yet allows partial views of bobbing heads in neighboring yards). Offers somewhat more privacy than a 4-foot fence.
- **The 6-foot fence.** The standard "privacy" fence and often the highest allowed by building codes. Reliably effective for privacy on flat terrain.

CREATING PLANS

TIME TO HIT THE DRAWING BOARD. Start with a camera, and take some shots of your property from different angles and depths. Drive stakes in the ground along the intended fence line, and then stretch a string line between them at the planned height of the fence. Include this mock-up in your photos.

Print out the best photos in 5" × 7" or 8" × 10" format, and then use a marker to draw your fence on the images. Repeat as needed until you feel comfortable with the results. Pay particular attention to the gate or entry sections as well as potential obstructions in the fence line (such as trees or existing gardens).

Note: If you haven't done so already, now is a good time to have utility lines marked on your property (see Before You Start Digging on page 29). If you do have buried lines to contend with, mark their locations on your site plan drawing, and adjust your post layout accordingly.

Use a 50- or 100-foot tape measure to measure the length of the fence lines. On a sheet of paper, make a rough plan drawing with the dimensions. If you are planning a gate, be sure to note its location and size.

Refine your initial sketches. Then create scaled drawings that plot the plan view (the overhead or bird's-eye perspective), the elevation (side view), and details (such as post ornamentation). Drawings allow you to work out important dimensions, confront potential obstacles, and calculate the quantity of materials. You can also use these drawings to obtain a building permit, if necessary.

Graph paper makes it easy to scale your drawings. Paper with a ¼" grid is a good size. Use it to scale your designs such that ¼" on paper equals 1 foot of actual distance. A ruler will help you to draw straight and accurate lines.

....

Scale and Proportion

An architect or landscape designer could lecture for hours on the applications of scale and proportion in fence design, but here I'll just slip you the crib sheet:

Scale: Make sure your fence isn't too big or small for the house, keeping in mind that proximity matters. A fence that's closer, taller, and/or more solid (dense or massive) has greater impact than a fence that's farther away, shorter, and/or lighter.

Proportion: Use a simplified version of the ancient "golden section" design formula to calculate things like post spacing and the overall shape of your fenced area(s). The proportion ratio is roughly 5:8 (or 1:1.6). That means if your fence is 5 feet tall, the posts should be spaced 8 feet apart. A 6-foot fence looks best with posts spaced 10 feet apart.

If the footprint of your fenced area is square, you're in good shape. If it's rectangular, try to stay within the limits of the 5:8 ratio — for example, a 50-foot wide area should be no more than 80 feet long (if possible). The reason is that a square or nicely proportioned rectangular area feels like a room, while a long, narrow area can feel more like a hallway.

....

DRAWING PLANS IN THREE STEPS

1. **Begin with a rough outline,** establishing the length of the fence.

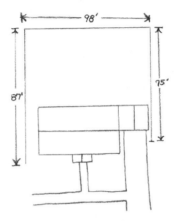

2. **Prepare a plan view,** drawn to scale, establishing the post spacing. Note that the standard on-center spacing here is 10 feet, with adjustments made at the back corners (alternatively, you can space all the posts equally, at less than 10 feet).

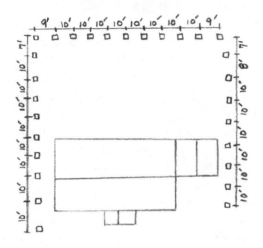

3. **Finally, create an elevation** of one or more fence sections, identifying the materials to be used and their length and location.

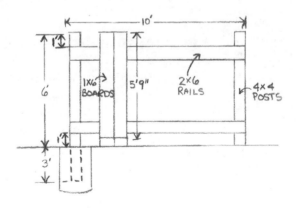

Dealing with Slopes

IF YOUR FENCE COVERS sloping ground, measure the slope's grade to determine which style of framing to use for the fence. If you decide to use a stepped framing technique, you should also work out the size of each fence section. For most do-it-yourselfers, it's easiest to measure slope with a water level (see page 25).

Chart the slope on your graph paper: Draw a level baseline along the bottom, then plot the run and rise, and then draw a line to indicate the slope. Lay some tracing paper over the drawing and divide the fence into sections with equally spaced posts. Use these drawings to help decide which of the following framing methods will work best.

Stepped framing. Works well on gradual slopes. Calculate the rise of each section by counting the total sections and dividing the rise (in inches) by the number of sections. The

Trees and Other Obstructions

Ideally your fence line is not interrupted by trees or other obstacles. But if it is, you can pass around the obstacle with a little bump-out in the fence, or you can incorporate the obstacle. However, don't fasten a fence to a tree; over time, this can damage both the tree and the fence. Instead, place a post several feet away at either side of the trunk, then let the rails and infill overhang the posts enough to fill in the gap.

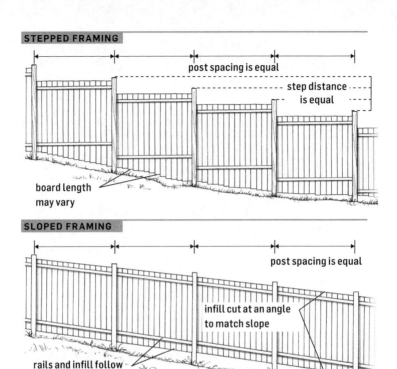

STEPPED FRAMING

post spacing is equal

step distance is equal

board length may vary

SLOPED FRAMING

post spacing is equal

infill cut at an angle to match slope

rails and infill follow contour of slope

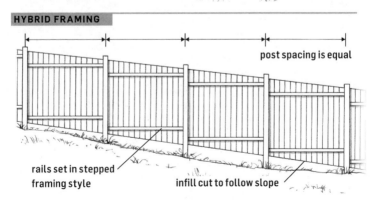

HYBRID FRAMING

post spacing is equal

rails set in stepped framing style

infill cut to follow slope

end result looks best with evenly spaced posts and an equal distance between the tops of the posts and the infill.

Sloped framing. The fence mirrors the slope. A good choice for steep slopes or rolling terrain.

Hybrid framing. Employs stepped framing, with the infill cut to match the slope. Best for very steep slopes.

PLUMB, LEVEL, AND SQUARE

THE BASIC CARPENTRY PRINCIPLES OF plumb and level are critical to fence building. Let's start with the essential terminology:

Plumb means perfectly vertical. A plumb post maximizes the force of gravity by transferring its load straight down to the earth. Any deviation from plumb weakens that force, and it also looks bad.

Level means perfectly horizontal; that is, to the horizon.

Square refers to a 90-degree corner, or a square or rectangular frame made up of four 90-degree corners.

Post Levels

A post level quickly straps to wood posts (or magnetizes to metal) and has three vials for quickly checking for plumb at a glance. This tool is simple to use and is very handy if you're working alone. However, its small size means limited accuracy.

Using a Carpenter's Level

Checking for plumb and level requires only one tool: the simple carpenter's level. The single best tool for fence building is a 4-foot level, while a 2-footer can be especially handy at times. Keep in mind that a level provides a read only on the surface on which it's placed. Generally speaking, the longer the level, the more accurate the reading. I like to set posts using two carpenter's levels, attaching them to adjacent sides with Velcro strips. This allows me to keep an eye on all four plumb vials before bracing the post.

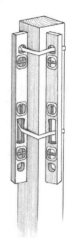

CHECK A POST FOR PLUMB with levels on two adjacent sides.

To transfer level lines from one post to the next, strap a level onto the edge of a *straight* 2×4 that's longer than the post spacing. Hold one end of the 2×4 on your reference line, raise or lower the other end until the bubble centers in the middle vial, then mark the spot on the other post.

Using a Water Level

A water level is a traditional, effective, and cheap tool for finding level over long distances. It's nothing more than a hose or long tube filled with water. The water levels itself at both ends of the hose, no matter how many twists and turns the tubing makes.

You can make a water level with any length of ⅜" or 5⁄16" clear vinyl tubing. Alternatively, you can use a garden hose that is fitted with water-level ends (available at home centers and hardware stores). There are even versions that beep to indicate level, which is handy when you are working alone. One warning about water levels: If one part sits in the shade and another part sits in direct sunlight for a long period of time, the water temperature (and, thus, the water density) will differ between the two areas, producing misleading results.

To use a water level, make sure there are no air bubbles or kinks in the tubing, and keep the ends open. Set one end of the tubing so that the water level aligns with the reference you have previously marked. Then place the other end of the tubing in the desired location. Once the water stabilizes, the water level at one end will be level with the water level of the other end.

Laser Levels

For fence building, a laser level is the high-tech alternative to a water level. Small handheld versions are pretty affordable these days (and they'll likely prove useful for future jobs around the house). But laser levels are not effective when leveling over long distances, especially outdoors. A better option is to rent a professional-grade rotary laser level. These levels can send a beam up to 100 feet and include a sensor unit that detects the beam, meaning that bright outdoor light will not interfere with the visibility of the laser light. Laser units with a self-leveling feature simplify setup. Regardless, make sure you get a tutorial before leaving the rental center.

DETERMINING SLOPE WITH A WATER LEVEL

Slope is a measure of *rise* (vertical distance) over *run* (horizontal distance).

1. Drive a wood stake at both the top and bottom of the slope.

2. Align the waterline at one end of the level with the top of the stake at the top of the hill.

3. Hold the other end of the level next to the stake at the bottom of the hill, and mark the position of the water line on the stake.

4. Measure the height of the stake at the top of the hill (a). Then measure the distance between the ground and the waterline mark on the stake at the bottom of the hill (b). Subtract (a) from (b). The result is the total rise (the vertical change) of the slope.

5. Find the run (the horizontal change) between the posts by measuring the level distance between them.

6. Transfer your findings to your layout drawing.

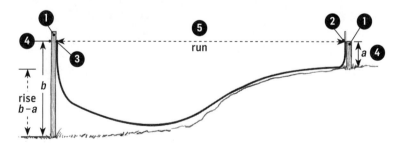

Plotting Right Angles

If your fence line needs to turn a corner, in most cases you will want the turn to create a perfect right angle. The easiest way to do this is to use the 3-4-5 technique (otherwise known as the Pythagorean theorem: $a^2 + b^2 = c^2$). Measure along one side of the fence line and make a mark at 3 feet, then measure along the perpendicular side and mark at 4 feet. Finally, measure the diagonal between the marks. If the distance is 5 feet, the corner is square. You can scale up the numbers for greater accuracy. For example, 6-8-10 or 9-12-15.

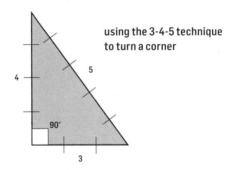

using the 3-4-5 technique to turn a corner

BEFORE YOU START DIGGING

MOST FENCES REQUIRE that you dig some holes for the posts. Before you pick up your shovel, however, make sure that you know what you are likely to encounter underground. Drainpipes; water and gas supply lines; septic tanks and drainage fields; and cables for electrical supply, telephone, and cable or satellite TV are all frequently buried. Knowing if you have any such underground obstacles on your property — and, if so, exactly where they are — is information that you as a homeowner should have, regardless of whether you are building a fence. Although there is not necessarily any problem with building a fence that passes over a buried cable or pipe, you certainly do not want to encounter such objects when you dig your postholes.

Having your lines marked now is easier than ever before: Pick up your phone and dial 811 (in the United States) to reach the national "Call Before You Dig" hotline. Your call will be routed to a local One Call Center. Explain the details of your project to the center operator, and the center will notify all of your local utility companies with lines on your property. Within a few days, a representative will come out and mark your lines — for free.

CHAPTER TWO

WOOD FENCES

Humankind has been constructing fences out of wood for thousands of years, and I'm happy to report that this is one of those things we seem to be improving on rather than messing up. Wood is accessible, affordable, and easy to shape and repair, and wood fences can be adapted to just about any style. They can also be strong, and with proper planning and care can last a long time. Perhaps best of all, building a durable and attractive wood fence does not require advanced carpentry skills.

CHOOSING THE WOOD

WOOD CAN LAST for a long, long time under controlled circumstances. Although all wood decays when it is outdoors, some types of wood withstand decay better than others. Choose wisely or you might invest time and money in a structure that is destined for the compost pile too soon after it is completed.

Cedar and Redwood

The most widely available decay-resistant woods today are cedar and redwood, both of which are lightweight, dimensionally stable, and attractive. Either of them is good material for fence infill boards. Most fence builders use pressure-treated lumber (see page 32) for the posts.

While you often pay a premium for cedar or redwood, you may not be getting what you think you're paying for. Even well-meaning lumber dealers tout the rot-resistance of these woods as though it was a given fact, but it isn't. As a tree matures its core changes from sapwood to heartwood. Such a change means that the core no longer conducts sap nor contains living cells. In cedar and redwood (and some other species), the heartwood contains extractives that are naturally decay-resistant. But it's important to note that the sapwood of cedar and redwood is really no more resistant to fungi and insects than any other wood species. If you want decay resistance, you need to choose lumber that contains all, or at least a high percentage of, heartwood.

Cedar and redwood lumber that contains most or all heartwood often is graded as "heart" or "all-heart" and tends to be the highest grade. As the grades descend, the lumber typically contains more and more sapwood and less heartwood. Ask your lumber supplier about what's available, and choose the best product for your project and budget. You can learn more about redwood grading on the California Redwood Association's (CRA) website (see Resources, page 120).

Pressure-Treated Wood

Pressure treating is a factory process in which chemical preservatives are pushed deep into the wood cells. This process imparts reliable decay resistance to inexpensive and fast-growing species, such as pine. Pressure-treated (PT) lumber offers an attractive balance of durability, strength, and low cost, making it the best choice for wood fence posts. It can be stained (or painted) to help it blend with the fence panel materials. If left untreated, PT lumber turns gray over time, just like redwood and cedar. *Note:* PT posts must be rated for "ground contact," meaning they're a suitable grade for burial.

In years past, PT lumber was treated with chromated copper arsenate (CCA), which contains arsenic. This treatment has been out of use in consumer lumber products for some time. Today's standard treatments do not contain arsenic and are generally considered to be less toxic than CCA. Even so, it's a good idea to wear a mask or respirator and gloves when cutting and working with treated lumber, and you should never burn scraps of the material.

Newer treatment chemicals can quickly corrode many types of fasteners, so it's important to use only hot-dipped galvanized or stainless fasteners (see page 34), or proprietary fasteners guaranteed for use with your type of lumber. When in doubt, consult a good lumber dealer.

Tips for Choosing Boards

When shopping for fence boards (1×4s, 1×6s, or other sizes), all you really need to know is that looks matter. Straight, clean boards with a few small, tight knots cost more than boards with large, loose knots, holes, and a bit of crookedness.

Flat-sawn or flat-grain boards have growth rings that are nearly parallel to the face of the board and are more likely to warp. Quarter-sawn or vertical-grain boards have growth rings that are nearly perpendicular to the face of the board and are less likely to warp.

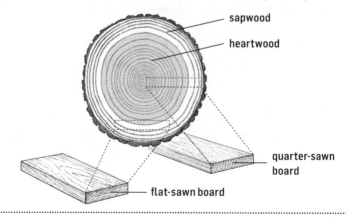

sapwood

heartwood

quarter-sawn board

flat-sawn board

Application

Perhaps more important than the lumber's natural resistance is where the wood will be located and how it will be used. Wood that is kept away from ground contact and is cleaned and coated with a water-repellent sealer regularly will last much longer than wood set on the ground and left unfinished. For most fence styles, decay resistance is the top priority when shopping for posts. For other parts of the fence, balance your finish and maintenance commitment with the level of weather resistance offered by the wood.

FASTENERS FOR ALL SEASONS

THE TWO PRINCIPAL CONCERNS with exterior-grade fasteners are corrosion resistance and holding power. Fasteners that rust will discolor a fence and eventually disintegrate, and those that are too weak for the job will jeopardize the standing (literally speaking!) of the fence you build.

Corrosion Resistance

Hot-dipped (HD) galvanized nails are the best choice for most fences. These fasteners offer good durability at a decent cost. Electroplated or electrogalvanized (EG) and hot galvanized (HG) nails also have a galvanized finish, but they don't stand up to the elements as well as HD products and typically are not recommended for use with pressure-treated lumber.

Stainless-steel nails are pricey, but they can be worth their weight in gold when building in damp or salty environments (along the coast, for example). Stainless steel is highly recommended for use with redwood or cedar, which contain tannic acids that react with galvanized and other types of fasteners, resulting in ugly stains (staining can be a factor even on a painted fence).

Manufacturers offer two grades of stainless steel: Type 304 is the standard, while type 316 has a bit more nickel, which stands up better to a salty environment. As for cost, the same fasteners that cost you $10 in galvanized will cost about $25 in stainless.

When choosing screws, look for those with either stainless steel or a galvanized finish and a weatherproof resin. I have not had great success using low-cost "decking screws" with a yellow zinc coating. In my experience, this coating seems to chip off or wear through as soon as the screw is driven into the wood.

Holding Power

Holding power relates to how well a fastener keeps wood parts held together as the wood swells and shrinks with moisture levels. It's hard to beat screws for holding power, and they make it easy to disassemble parts of a fence, if necessary. Ring-shank or spiral-shank nails are a good choice if you prefer to use nails. Nails with smooth shanks offer the least holding power and are prone to popping. For fastening pickets and fence boards, I typically use top-quality HD galvanized ring-shank wood siding nails that have been double dipped in zinc. But I would certainly use stainless steel if I were working with redwood or cedar, or if I didn't plan to paint the wood.

Other Hardware

Some fences require heavy-duty brackets or fasteners, such as carriage bolts or lag screws. Carriage bolts are set in a pre-drilled hole and secured with a nut. The head has a smooth, round finish and goes on the most visible side of the connection. Lag screws do not require a nut and are not quite as strong as carriage bolts. But they are often a better choice than normal screws for attaching large rails to posts. Again, stick with stainless steel or hot-dipped galvanized materials. Electroplated bolts (identified by their shiny surface) tend to rust quickly.

SETTING POSTS

POSTS ARE THE BASIC structural component of most fences. Wood posts can be used with both wood and metal fences. Depending on the fence design, posts can be a prominent visual element or barely noticeable. Regardless, they always serve a critical function. Set the posts right, and the rest of the fence building will be easier and more rewarding. Set the posts wrong, and you will regret the errors for a long time. Setting the posts right means placing them in a straight line, spacing them evenly and properly, embedding them securely in the ground, and positioning them perfectly plumb.

Size and Spacing

The size of posts and the spacing between them often are aesthetic decisions, but first and foremost they are structural factors. Keep in mind that your local building code may have minimal requirements other than those given here.

There are two categories of fence posts. Terminal posts are located on both sides of the gate, at all corners, and at the ends. Because these posts generally carry the heaviest load and receive the most abuse, they should be set deeper into the ground and often should be sized larger than the intermediate posts, as shown in the illustration.

POST SIZE AND SPACING

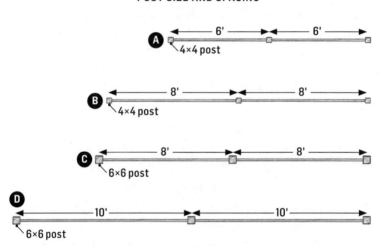

A. Tight spacing, nicely proportioned for short and tall fencing. Can handle heavy infill.

B. Most common post size and spacing. A good choice for rail fences and other light-infill styles.

C. Strong size and spacing combination. A good choice for heavy vertical-board fences or other styles that showcase the framing.

D. Strong but graceful spacing. Suitable for nearly any fence style.

Fence Post Rules of Thumb

- Use only pressure-treated wood that is rated for ground contact. Budget permitting, consider "premium" PT posts with a water-repellent factory finish.

- Choose the posts yourself. Eyeball each one lengthwise to find the straightest specimens. Avoid posts with excessive splitting, checking, or knotholes.

- Buy posts a little longer than you need and cut them to length later. Setting posts so their tops are perfectly aligned is a very difficult and frustrating task. For the same reason, avoid posts with precut decorative tops. You can easily add decorative tops after the posts are set and the tops have been cut straight.

- When in doubt about post size, go bigger. Oversized posts aren't a problem; undersized posts are.

- Bury posts as deeply as reasonably possible.

Footings

The footing is the all-important connection of the post to the earth. There are several ways to form a footing. Each has its pros and cons, and none has an iron-clad guarantee of perfection. I won't try to convince you to set your posts one way or the other, but I will help you make an educated decision.

First and foremost, posts must be buried in the ground — and the deeper, the better. Decks are built with posts set in metal bases attached to concrete piers, but this is not a good way to handle fence posts because they need the lateral support that deep burial affords. Likewise, I would not set fence posts in metal brackets that are hammered into the ground. I have my mailbox installed using one of these, but it is not what I consider a solid connection.

COMPARING BACKFILL CHOICES

The next questions involve how deep to dig the holes, how wide, and what materials to use as backfill. The traditional choices for backfilling include alternating layers of tamped earth and gravel, filling the holes with concrete, or using a combination of tamped earth and gravel plus concrete. The depth and width of the postholes are based on the type of footing material.

Earth-and-gravel footings (or earth alone) require relatively slim holes (roughly twice the width of the posts), which reduces digging time. The only expense involved is for a bit of gravel, as the earth component can come from the dirt that you dig out of the hole. The posts also can be dug up easily for future repairs.

Earth-and-gravel footings work best in relatively dry, undisturbed soil that compacts well. This footing is less effective in light soil that contains a lot of sand or organic material; soil that has been disturbed (that is, dug up and backfilled before); or heavy soil that contains a lot of clay. Heavy soil drains poorly and loses much of its strength and holding power when wet.

Setting posts in concrete is a reasonable option in most conditions, but especially when the soil is less than ideal. It generally takes less time to set posts in concrete than it does to set posts in earth and gravel (backfilling and tamping of earth and gravel can be time consuming). On the downside, the holes must be wider.

Understanding Frost Heave

In cold climates, concrete footings are prone to the powerful effects of frost heave. The colder it gets, the more the moisture in the soil will freeze and expand. This force exerts enough pressure underground to lift houses and roads, not to mention fence posts. The simpler-said-than-done antidote to frost heave is to set the bottoms of footings below the **frost line**, the deepest point at which frost is likely to form. Your local building department can give you the local frost depth and may require you to set posts at or below this level. In some climates, digging below the frost line can require holes that are 4, 5, or even 6 feet deep.

Frost heave is the subject of ongoing debate. Some experts recommend placing one-third of the buried portion below the frost line (for example, 4½-foot deep burial for a 3-foot frost line). Others point to the lateral forces pushing against the side of a footing, as well as the pressure from below, and claim that a deeper footing is more prone to heaving. In any case, there are no guarantees.

Frost heave can affect any type of footing, but my instincts tell me that earth-and-gravel footings would fare better than concrete, due to the latter's larger surface against which frost heave forces can push. Even if I'm wrong about this, at the very least earth-and-gravel footings make it much easier to reset any dislocated posts.

My general recommendation is to bury at least one-third of the overall length of the posts. For a 6-foot finished fence, bury the posts 3 feet (using 9-foot posts). This means the holes must be about 3½ feet deep to allow for a bottom layer of gravel. With good soil conditions and careful attention to detail, short picket fences 3 to 4 feet tall could be supported by posts buried no less than 2 feet deep in holes that extend an additional 6" for gravel.

For terminal posts (posts at the gate, corners, and ends), the strongest installation is to set them in concrete 6" to 12" below the frost line, regardless of which technique you use with the other footings.

POST PRESSURES

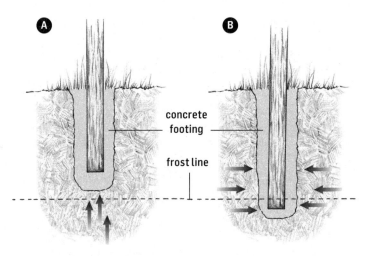

If a post footing is not set below the frost line (A), the ground can freeze and expand beneath the footing, pushing it up. Even when the bottom of the footing is below the frost line (B), lateral soil pressure can loosen the footing unless it is buried very deep.

For a 4×4 post, for example, you'll need a 12"-diameter hole for a concrete footing versus an 8"-diameter hole for an earth-and-gravel footing. Also, encasing any kind of wood in concrete can lead to premature rot and/or insect infestation (namely carpenter ants). Concrete is porous and can trap water around the post, and seasonal wood shrinkage allows additional water in through the gap between the post and the footing at ground level (though this can be reduced by shaping the concrete so that it sheds water away from the post and by sealing the joint with caulk).

DIGGING HOLES

For many do-it-yourselfers, no part of fence building is more difficult and discouraging than digging deep, narrow, straight, nicely aligned holes in the ground. There are a few basic options for tackling this job. You've marked your utility lines, right? (See Before You Start Digging on page 29.)

Manual digging. A garden spade is the best manual tool for breaking through sod and getting a hole started. But once you get down a foot or so, switch to a clamshell digger. Hold the digger with the handles together and stab it into the hole. Spread

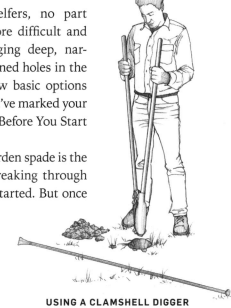

USING A CLAMSHELL DIGGER

the handles apart and carefully lift out the dirt. If you run into large rocks or hard soil, use a digging bar, which is a 6-foot solid steel (or iron) bar with a chisel-like blade on one end and a tamping head (handy for backfilling the hole) on the other. A digging bar is also useful for loosening soil before removing it with a shovel or posthole digger.

As you dig, pile the dirt on a piece of plastic or in a wheelbarrow or garden cart. Don't make the holes any wider than necessary. With earth-and-gravel footings, part of the strength

---

Tools for Tough Digging

- The NU Boston Digger is similar to a clamshell digger, but one handle has a lever that operates a scoop on the bottom for dirt removal. Pros use these in the famously hard, rocky earth of New England.

- Tackle really hard soil by pouring water into the hole and letting it soak in for a few hours or overnight. It's muddy, messy work, but easier than hacking through hard soil.

- Cut out tree roots with a pruning saw or a reciprocating saw equipped with a special pruning blade.

- Consider your options if you run into bedrock (or ledge): Sometimes you can chip away at the rock with a digging bar and create a hole deep and wide enough to hold some concrete for the post. Another option is to drill a hole in the ledge, cement a rod or pin in the hole, and secure the post to the rod. (Consult a pro about this option.)

---

comes from leaving the surrounding soil undisturbed. With concrete footings, the wider the hole, the more concrete it needs. Aim for holes that are as close to cylindrical as possible. And keep a close eye on your fence line: you want the centers of all holes to be aligned as closely as possible.

Power augering. Using a power auger can be much faster than manual digging, which is not to imply it makes the job easy. Tool rental stores usually have at least one type of power auger available. Be sure to select an auger bit that matches the depth and diameter of the holes you need to dig. Often, the biggest bit you can find is 3 feet long and 8" in diameter. If you need to dig 12"-wide holes, you can rock the auger back and

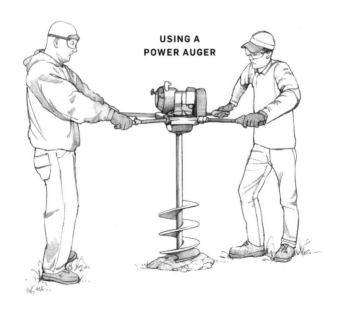

USING A POWER AUGER

forth a little as it works itself deeper into the hole. (In truth, you may not have any choice on this because most rental stores do not carry larger diameter bits.)

There are both one- and two-person power augers available. One-person augers with the engine mounted on top of the tool scare me, and I would not use one. Two-person versions of the same design are much safer and easier to use, but it's still backbreaking work that requires careful attention and a good grip on the machine.

If you must work alone, a flexible-shaft auger is worth looking for. The engine is separated from the auger, making it fairly easy to handle. You may need a trailer hitch to tow the tool home.

Drill into soil as though you're drilling a deep hole in wood or metal: Advance into the hole a little, then withdraw the bit to clear the loose debris, then advance a little more. Also, do not try to clear big rocks with the auger; use a digging bar for that work. Finally, take regular breaks.

Hiring out the digging. The last option for digging holes is my favorite. Hire someone with an auger accessory that they mount on a truck, tractor, or skid-steer loader, and let them dig the holes quickly while you sip lemonade. Yes, you have to write a check to get these holes dug, but it may be a smaller amount than you anticipate. This strategy works only if the vehicle can get to the site. You might have to hunt a bit for the contractor; contact local fence-building contractors, or talk to local farmers or building contractors for recommendations.

PREPARING THE HOLE

Ideally, every posthole will be at least 30" deep and preferably 12" or more below the frost line. In the real world, however, some of the holes may not be as deep as you would like due to obstacles such as immovable rocks. It's not a catastrophe to leave a hole or two short, but always strive for at least 2 feet of depth. Just don't deviate on the depth of the holes for terminal posts. Make an extra effort to create an adequate hole, and if that's not feasible, consider relocating the post.

With all the holes dug, set up your string lines again to check the alignment. Add a 6" layer of crushed rock into the bottom of each hole — for any type of footing. Start with 4" of rock, tamp it well with a 2×4, then add 2" more after the post has been set in the hole and braced. The rock allows water that reaches the bottom of the post to drain away. One caveat: if the surrounding soil is regularly on the wet side, you might not want to use gravel; this material can actually attract water to the base of the post.

BRACING AND PLUMBING POSTS

Use your string lines to help align the posts as you set them. With 4×4 posts, simply move the string lines 4" to one side, then make sure the face of each post remains ½" away from the string line (a 4×4 post measures 3½" × 3½"). The ½" offset prevents the posts from interfering with the string. Posts must be perfectly plumb and securely braced before you backfill or add concrete. There are two ways to do this, both of which are much more easily done if you enlist a helper.

Shim bracing. This simple technique works for earth-and-gravel backfill. It requires cutting at least four bracing shims that are sized to fit the space between the posts and the surrounding hole edges. For 8" holes and 4×4 posts, use a 30" length of 1×6 (or ½" plywood). Cut the piece of wood in half lengthwise, then cut two shims from each of the boards.

Center a post in its hole and hold it plumb with a level while your partner slips one shim into the hole directly under the level and another shim on the opposite side. Move the level to an adjacent side and repeat the process. Begin backfilling the hole, tamping as you go. When the backfill nearly reaches the bottoms of the shims, carefully remove them to finish filling the hole.

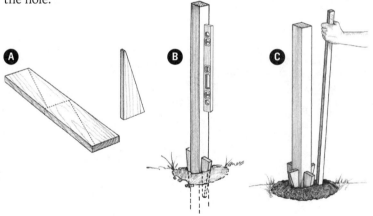

ONE 30" 1×6 yields two shims for bracing 4×4 posts; cut four, total (A). Set the first two shims on opposite sides of the post, keeping the post plumb. Do the same thing on the remaining two sides (B). Backfill the hole with crushed rock and earth. Avoid disturbing the shims (C).

Lumber bracing. Traditional bracing is better than the shim method when you have wide holes or are backfilling with concrete. I usually use 1×4s for braces. For posts that will be 6 feet or more above ground level, use 8-foot-long braces. You need two braces at each post, along with stakes hammered into the ground. Use 1×2s for stakes, cutting one end to a point.

Center the post at its hole and hold it plumb. Place one brace at an angle alongside the post. Drive a stake into the ground alongside the bottom of the brace, and then drive a nail or screw through the brace into the stake. Check the post for plumb with a level on the side facing the stake, and then drive a screw through the brace and into the post. Repeat with another brace placed at a right angle to the first.

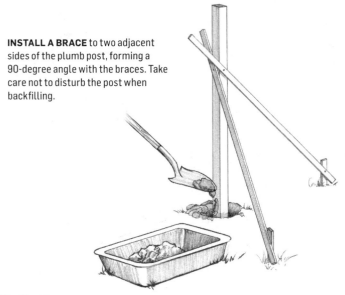

INSTALL A BRACE to two adjacent sides of the plumb post, forming a 90-degree angle with the braces. Take care not to disturb the post when backfilling.

INSTALLING EARTH-AND-GRAVEL FOOTINGS

Earth (soil) and gravel work together to provide stability and drainage. The keys to success with this type of footing are alternating layers of each material and tamping each layer to ensure a well-compacted and snug bed for the post.

It's important to use the right kind of gravel. Crushed rock has jagged edges and is ideal for drainage at the bottom of the hole; the jagged edges create large voids that allow water to pass through quickly. Crushed rock is often screened and graded for size; the larger the rocks, the better the drainage. Be sure to tamp it thoroughly.

The best gravel for the backfill layers is bank-run gravel, or bank gravel (which also works for the hole bottoms). It's a mix of rounded large and small rocks that compact nicely but also drain well. If bank-run gravel is hard to find, pea gravel (a graded product of fairly small gravel) is a suitable alternative and can usually be found in small bags at home centers and garden suppliers.

With the post sitting on a level layer of gravel, braced and plumb, add another 2" of gravel in the hole. Tamp the gravel well, and then shovel in about 4" of soil. Tamp that layer, and then add more gravel. Continue this work until the hole is filled.

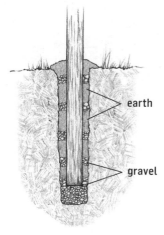

EARTH-AND-GRAVEL FOOTING

You can tamp with a 2×4, but a digging bar with a tamping head on one end is better for the tight confines of a posthole. Regardless of the tool you use, try to avoid hitting the post. Work your way little by little around the post as you tamp, rather than trying to tamp one side completely before moving to another. Tamp each layer as much as possible, periodically checking the post to make sure it stays plumb. If it shifts during backfilling, you may have to adjust your bracing and possibly remove some dirt and gravel before resuming. The more material that fills the hole, the more immovable the post becomes.

Overfill the top layer with dirt and compact it carefully to create a slope away from the post. This encourages water to drain away from both the post and the hole. This top layer may need to be refreshed from time to time with some fresh dirt and a renewed slope.

USING CONCRETE FOOTINGS

If you plan to set your fence posts in concrete, you must decide whether or not to mix your own concrete and, if so, how to do it.

Ordering ready-mix concrete. Sometimes it makes sense to have ready-mix concrete delivered by truck. Depending on the job, ready-mix can save time and be not much more costly

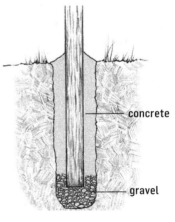

CONCRETE FOOTING

than the alternatives. Ready-mix is ordered by the cubic yard; a yard is typically the minimal amount you must order. One cubic yard equals 27 cubic feet (or 46,656 cubic inches). Assuming that your 4×4 posts are going into 36"-deep × 12"-diameter holes that have 6" of gravel in the bottom, then a yard of concrete can fill about 15½ holes. However, plan on it filling 13 or 14 holes to allow some extra for a bit of overfilling for each hole, inevitable spills, and a small safety margin.

Have all your posts braced and ready before the concrete truck arrives, and make sure the truck can get fairly close to the holes without driving through your yard. Also have a small crew ready to help, equipped with shovels and a couple of wheelbarrows. If you keep the truck waiting too long while you work to unload it, you may have to pay extra for that idle time.

The typical process for unloading ready-mix involves sliding a wheelbarrow under the truck's chute, filling it with a manageable amount of concrete, wheeling over to the hole, and shoveling in the concrete. The process then repeats until the holes are filled. Helpers can work a second wheelbarrow as well as finish the tops of the filled holes.

Mixing your own concrete with a power mixer. If you have a lot of holes to fill but prefer a more leisurely pace, rent an electric or gas-powered concrete mixer. Although you can throw bags of concrete mix (premixed concrete) into the mixer, it is cheaper to mix your own dry ingredients: 1 part portland cement, 2 parts sand, and 3 parts coarse gravel. The dry ingredients are sold at some lumberyards, home centers, and through masonry materials suppliers. Add the dry ingredients into the mixer, and then slowly add water until you reach the right consistency. When you can form a small pile of concrete that holds its shape, the mixture is ready to use. If water starts pooling on the surface of the mix, it's too wet. Dump the mixed concrete into a wheelbarrow. If available, use a mixer that can dump directly into the postholes. The clock starts ticking as soon as you add water to the mix (or the concrete truck arrives). Concrete begins hardening in 45 minutes, or less in warm weather.

Using bags of premixed concrete. For fewer holes, it's easiest to buy bags of concrete mix. Empty the contents into a mortar tub or wheelbarrow, add a little water, and mix the ingredients with a hoe (a mortar hoe, which has two holes in its blade, is the best tool for this, but a standard garden hoe works just fine). Bagged concrete comes in 40- to 90-pound bags. One large bag yields about ⅔ cubic feet.

Use only full bags to ensure the proper proportions, and mix the dry ingredients well before adding water as directed. Start with about 90 percent of the recommended amount of water, and then add small amounts as needed until you reach the right consistency (able to hold its own shape without water pooling on the surface).

FINISH THE CONCRETE SURFACE to create a dome that promotes drainage.

Pouring and finishing the concrete. Overfill each hole slightly, and then use a margin trowel or a putty knife to mound the top into a smooth dome that will shed water away from the post. Leave the post undisturbed for at least two days. When the concrete has cured, apply a bead of clear silicone caulk at the joint between the post and concrete. Renew the caulk anytime you start to see a gap developing at the joint.

PREPARING HYBRID FOOTINGS

Some fence builders have found that a footing that combines concrete with tamped earth and gravel stands up well to frost heave. Dig the holes about 12" below the frost line and shovel 6" of gravel in the hole. Brace the post in the hole and add a

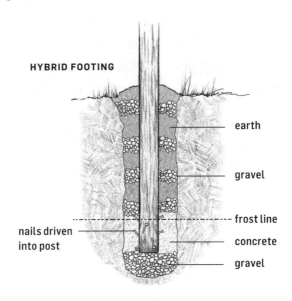

HYBRID FOOTING

earth

gravel

frost line

nails driven into post

concrete

gravel

2" layer of gravel. Now pour a 4-inch layer of concrete into the hole. When the concrete cures, fill the hole with alternating layers of earth and gravel, as described on page 49 (Installing Earth-and-Gravel Footings).

To better embed the post in the concrete, drive some large nails into each side of the post before pouring the concrete. Use hot-dipped galvanized or stainless-steel nails (16d or larger). Alternatively, you can insert short pieces of ½" rebar through holes you drill in the post.

How Much Concrete Do I Need?

To determine the amount of concrete you need for a posthole (or any other cylinder), begin by determining the volume of the hole:

radius^2 × depth of hole (in inches) × 3.14
= hole volume (in cubic inches)

Next, determine the volume of the post:

post length × post width × post height (below ground)
= post volume (in cubic inches)

Then, assuming the hole is a perfect cylinder (which it never is) and your measurements are exact (they might be close), determine your net hole volume:

hole volume – post volume
= net hole volume (in cubic inches)

This calculation tells you how much concrete is needed (ideally) to fill one hole to ground level. But you want to overfill each hole a bit to account for settling and for making a sloped top — meaning that you should add 5 or 10 percent to your estimate. And because mixed concrete is sold by the cubic foot rather than the cubic inch, divide your total by 1,728 (one cubic foot = 1,728 cubic inches).

After you have completed the calculations for a single hole, multiply the amount needed for one hole by the total number of holes. The result determines your total concrete needs.

Here's an example for a single typically sized hole:

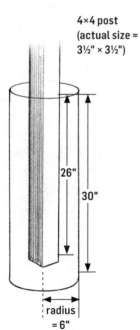

4×4 post
(actual size =
3½" × 3½")

hole volume: $6^2 \times 30 \times 3.14 =$
3,391.2 cubic inches

post volume: $3.5 \times 3.5 \times 26 =$
318.5 cubic inches

net hole volume:
$3,391.2 - 318.5 =$
3,072.7 cubic inches

volume of concrete needed plus 10%:
$3,072.7 + (3,072.7 \times .1) =$
$3,072.7 + 307.27 =$
3,379.97 cubic inches

volume of concrete needed in cubic feet:
$3,379.97 \div 1,728 =$
1.96 cubic feet per hole

26"

30"

radius
= 6"

ATTACHING RAILS

RAILS ARE THE CROSS-MEMBERS of a fence that span from post to post. In a basic post-and-rail fence, the rails constitute the entire infill and are therefore the principal visual element of the fence. In most other wood fence styles, the rails are primarily a structural element that stiffens the whole assembly and provides a surface for attaching infill boards or pickets.

To make a strong fence before metal fasteners were available, rails were passed through holes or mortises that were cut into or through the posts. Today rails typically are nailed or screwed onto posts.

Rail-Only Fences

The basic rail fence is a longtime fixture of rural life and remains a functional style for controlling horses and other animals. Rail-only fences are also popular for modest boundaries and garden markers. The standard construction method involves setting all of the posts along the fence line, then nailing the rails to the faces of the posts.

The height of the fence and the rail spacing are entirely up to you, although rail fences tend to be fairly low. The most common type of rail fence used for animal enclosure has 4×4 posts set on 8-foot centers, with three or four 1×6 horizontal rails evenly spaced. For decorative fences, two rails are often sufficient. You should be able to find boards that are 16 feet long, which can speed up installation. If you'd like to break up the horizontal lines of the fence a bit, consider adding one or more angled cross-rails.

Structural Rails

For rails that serve a strictly structural role, you can choose to install them either flat or on edge. Flat rails offer some symmetrical appeal and may simplify some types of fence construction, but generally I recommend installing the rails on edge. Flat rails are almost guaranteed to sag over time, as people tend to lean against or sit on rails. Infill boards add their own weight, which also encourages sag. If you're set on flat rails, consider using 4×4s for at least the bottom rail, then install the top rail to the tops of the posts. You can also reduce the span between posts to help minimize sagging.

COMPARATIVE RAIL STRENGTH

Rails set on edge allow greater post spacing. When the fence design requires rails to be mounted flat, strengthen the structure by reducing the distance between posts.

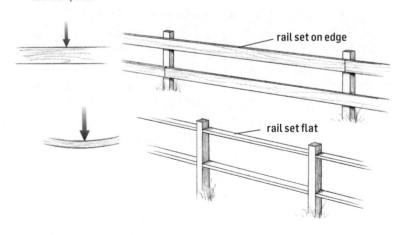

rail set on edge

rail set flat

Rails that are mounted on their edge also offer more choices for mounting infill boards or pickets. Often, the infill goes on the most visible side of the fence, meaning that you probably won't see the rails. Another option is to center the edge-mounted rails inside the posts so the infill is nearly flush with the faces of the posts, making the fence identical on both sides.

For a typical picket fence, plan for two rails. For a high fence, especially if it will be filled with boards, use three rails.

Options in Joinery

The strongest joints between rails and posts are those that use holes or mortises in the posts, especially if the rails are installed on edge. These joints require a lot of work to make. It takes time to cut the holes or mortises, and they must be aligned perfectly for the rails to fit correctly. Simpler joinery, such as butted joints or those that use metal brackets, requires less work and is more typical for standard board fences.

Through-mortised posts create a somewhat rustic fence that might need no additional fasteners. For this joinery style, I recommend using 6×6 posts, which can accommodate mortises for two 2×4 rails. To cut the mortises, mark the outline on the post, drill a fairly large hole through one corner of the layout, and use a long wood-cutting blade in a reciprocating saw to finish the cut. Alternatively, drill a series of closely spaced holes, then clean out the mortise with a chisel. Cut the rails about 2 feet longer than the distance between posts, and slip them into the mortises. You can use this technique to set rails flat or on edge.

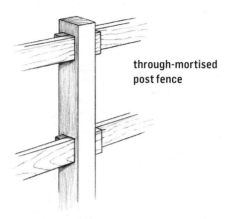

through-mortised post fence

Butt joints are the most common means of joining rails to posts. Rails are cut to fit exactly between the posts and are fastened with nails, screws, or special metal brackets. Fence brackets are inexpensive, are easy to install, and create a strong connection. They don't look great, but you can stain or paint them to blend with the fence (prime them first with a metal primer). If you use just nails or screws, drive them at an angle (called *toenailing*) through the rail and into the post. Drill pilot holes to prevent splitting the wood.

Face nailing is the quickest approach for installing rails on edge. Normally, the rails are attached to the back sides of the posts, with boards or pickets going on the other side. Again, drill pilot holes to prevent splitting. For strength combined with neat appearance, I like to set rails into notches that are cut into the posts.

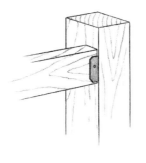

USING METAL BRACKETS. Metal brackets can secure a butt joint, with the rail on edge or flat.

FACE NAILING. When possible, use long boards that span to three posts, and stagger the joints so that they fall on alternate posts (see page 57).

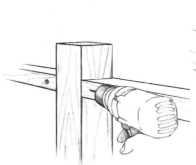

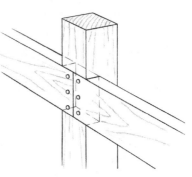

TOENAILING. Rail-to-post butt joints can be secured by nails driven at an angle through the rail and into the post. Drill pilot holes to prevent splitting.

NOTCHING AND FACE NAILING. This method creates stronger joints than face nailing alone.

Rail notches must be laid out and cut carefully for all the parts to fit together perfectly. The most foolproof (if not the most efficient) approach is to finish one post before moving on to the next.

1. Begin by marking a layout on the first post. Hold a piece of rail stock in place perpendicular to and across the face of a post. Make sure it is level, then use a pencil to mark its top and bottom edges on the post.

2. With a circular saw set
to cut exactly 1½" deep
(or the measured thick-
ness of the rail material),
make a series of closely
spaced passes between
the lines.

3. Use a hammer to knock
out pieces of cut wood,
then clean out the notch
with a chisel and ham-
mer. A flat wood rasp
might come in handy on
this chore as well.

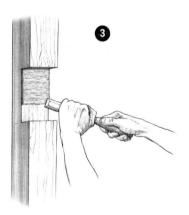

4. Test-fit the rail in the
notch, and adjust the
notch depth if necessary.
Place the next rail sec-
tion in the other side of
the notch and use a level
on the rail to guide the
layout for the notch on
the next post. Attach the
rails with nails or screws.

POST TOP DETAILS

DEPENDING ON THE DESIGN of your fence, the posts may be virtually inconspicuous, moderately noticeable, or prominently displayed. In any case, the post tops deserve special consideration. With lumber, the end grain area is the most vulnerable to water infiltration and damage. The end grain at the top end of a post is fully exposed to the elements and can soak up a lot of water over time. The simple solution is to cut the post tops at an angle (to promote drainage) or to cover the ends with plain or decorative post caps.

Cutting post tops, especially at an angle, can be a bit challenging. You can use a circular saw, a reciprocating saw, or a sharp handsaw; I prefer either of the power tools for this work. Use a level and a long 2×4 or a water level (see page 25) to establish a level line from post to post. If cutting at an angle, use a combination square or Speed Square to mark a consistent 45-degree line on both sides of the level line.

Using just a standard circular saw (with a 7¼" blade), set the blade depth to the deepest cut possible. Make one pass with the saw up one angled line, then move to the other side and cut down the other angled line. If you are very careful, the two passes will produce a reasonably clean surface. If one side is a bit higher than the other, trim a little more off the higher side.

With a reciprocating saw equipped with a long wood-cutting blade, you can make this cut with a single pass. Be warned that the blade of a reciprocating saw has a tendency to wander off-line a bit. Try to hold the saw at a consistent angle, keep the speed high, and move slowly through the post.

If you are not experienced with using either of these two types of saw, make practice cuts on a scrap 4×4. When cutting 6×6 posts, you can't cut to the center with a circular saw alone, meaning that using a reciprocating saw (or handsaw) is also mandatory.

Decorative Post Tops

Decorative post tops cover and protect the end grain while giving a special look to the fence. As mentioned, you can buy 4×4 posts with decorative features milled into them, but it's much easier to set longer-than-needed posts in the ground, and then trim them to finished height before adding the post tops. Most lumberyards and home centers stock a few post cap styles, or you can special-order for a wider selection.

Some prefabricated post caps have a screw in the end, so all you have to do is drill a pilot hole in the center of the post top and thread it in. Add a little exterior-grade adhesive to improve the strength of this connection. You can also make your own custom caps. Simple squares cut from 1×6 boards can serve as

A SQUARE WOOD CAP cut from a 1x6 board (for 4x4 posts) protects the post top. This cap is simple, effective, and just slightly decorative. Center the caps on the posts, and then fasten with exterior-grade adhesive and two galvanized ring-shank nails.

the basis for any number of finished tops. With a power miter saw or a table saw, you can produce uniformly sized pieces of wood trim very quickly. Cove or quarter-round molding adds a nice touch. Using a circular saw or a router, you can create a nice shadow line with a shallow cut.

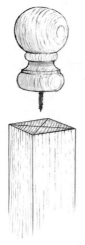

INSTALLING A DECORATIVE POST TOP

Find the center of the post by drawing straight lines from corner to corner. Drill a pilot hole at the intersection of the lines, add adhesive (if desired), and screw down the decorative top.

THE PICKET FENCE

PICKET FENCES ARE, by and large, front-yard fences. They mark the boundary between the private residence and the public street. They are intended to look nice, keep people from wandering into the yard, and perhaps offer a bit of protection to a garden. Picket fences typically are 3 to 4 feet tall, and the pickets lend themselves well to creative embellishment, allowing you to make a one-of-a-kind statement by designing a distinctive pattern or cut to the pickets.

Making Pickets

Pickets are normally made from 1×3 or 1×4 boards, although 1" to 1½" squares can work well, too. The tops can be flat but are usually cut in some decorative pattern both for looks and to help shed water from exposed end grain. You can buy pickets in a limited number of shapes and standard lengths from lumberyards and home centers. But if you're building your own picket fence, why not design and make your own? Even if you choose a standard picket style, making your own allows you to use good-quality wood and to customize the lengths to follow ground contours.

The quickest way to cut pickets with pointed or angled tops with a consistent length is to set up a power miter saw with a stop block. Adjust the saw to the proper angle, clamp or nail the stop block into place, and then start cutting. For pointed tops, cut one side of a board, flip it over, and cut the other. To create a pyramid-type shape on 1" to 1½" square pickets, make the same cut on all four sides.

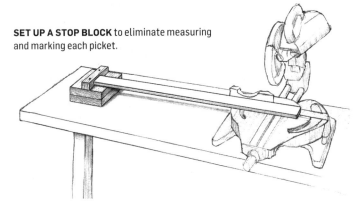

SET UP A STOP BLOCK to eliminate measuring and marking each picket.

For more elaborate designs that require pickets to be cut one at a time, make a template out of ¼" hardboard or plywood. Use the template to trace the design onto each board, and then make the cuts with a jigsaw or band saw (for curved cuts). Usually it's easiest to cut the pickets before installing them, but if the fence covers irregular terrain, you may want to install overly long pickets first, then cut them to length and trim them into their final shape.

To create a curved top edge to a section of pickets, it helps to have an uncomplicated design. Simply install the pickets, mark the layout, and make the cuts. To mark a curve, cut a thin strip of wood a little longer than the spacing between posts, bend the strip into the desired shape and tack it to the posts. Trace along the curved strip to mark the pickets for cutting.

Attaching Pickets

To install pickets with their tops level, the basic approach is to attach a string line from post to post and then align each picket with the string. For an alternating-height style, use more than one string line. If you plan to cut a shape along previously installed pickets, run all of the pickets a little long so each one gets a full cut.

Pickets may be all the same width and length, or they may have multiple widths and alternating lengths, depending on your design. In any case, I recommend uniformity of spacing between pickets. Irregular spacing tends to make the fence look like it was created haphazardly. Use a spacer board to set the gaps between pickets. For a traditional, relatively open look, use a spare picket for the spacer. For a bit more privacy, use a thinner spacer. An all-in-one picket jig lets you set the spacing and height at once.

Attach pickets to the rails with galvanized ring-shank nails. For 1× pickets and 2× rails — a total thickness of 2¼" — use 6d (2"-long) nails. Two nails at each rail junction should suffice. To be on the safe side, check the pickets with a level periodically to confirm they're plumb.

THE PICKET SPACING JIG

This simple device ensures that pickets are installed plumb, properly spaced, and at the correct height (and you can build it from scrap lumber). Use a framing square to make sure the block is perpendicular to the spacer board; if they're off, your pickets won't hang plumb.

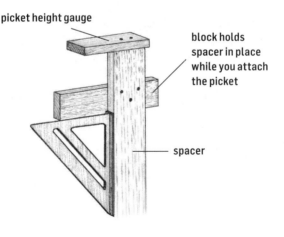

picket height gauge

block holds spacer in place while you attach the picket

spacer

VERTICAL-BOARD FENCES

VERTICAL-BOARD FENCES typically are higher than picket fences, with their boards more closely spaced. Thus, they are most often thought of as backyard fences, intended to ensure privacy, add some security, and keep kids and pets from wandering off. That said, there is no reason why boards cannot be treated like pickets, with decorative top cuts and with some spacing between boards to allow air currents and sunlight to pass through. This design also allows for seeing between the boards, if that is your intention. See the section on picket fences for suggestions on cutting and installing the boards (page 65).

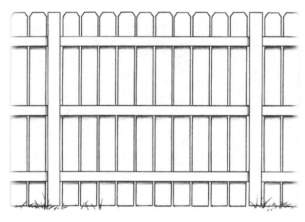

vertical-board fence

Boards for vertical-board fences can be purchased in standard sizes (typically 1×4, 1×6, or 1×8). These boards are attached to rails (preferably three rails for a high fence, two for a picket fence) and can be cut to size, if necessary, quite quickly. You can simply create a wall of solid boards, but to make a more stylistic fence, the board tops can be cut into points, clipped (dog-eared) at the corners, or rounded. Alternating widths of boards in either random or organized sequences can create a nice visual effect.

The board-on-board (or staggered) pattern is one I particularly like. Depending on how the boards are installed, this design can completely block views or offer slim glimpses from a right angle. At the same time, this design allows air to circulate and has a nice rhythmic look, with some contrast in light and shadow. It is also easy to build. Attach the boards with galvanized ring-shank nails or exterior-grade screws.

LOUVERED FENCES

Louvered fences are functionally much like the board-on-board style previously mentioned. They offer substantial privacy, yet still allow air to pass through. I think they look best around houses with modern architectural design. Louvered boards, typically either 1×4s or 1×6s, can be installed either horizontally or vertically. Both styles require careful layout and installation. Louvered fences use more wood and take longer to build than a flat style of board fence. Unless you have a strong reason for doing otherwise, I suggest placing the louvered boards at a 45-degree angle.

Installing Louvers

When installing 1×4 or 1×6 louvered boards horizontally, space the posts no more than 6 feet apart. (However, stay away from this style altogether if you think it might inspire someone to try to climb over this type of fence.) Metal brackets made specifically for attaching louvered fence boards to posts are the best way to handle horizontal boards, but you can also use wood spacers (see illustration on page 72).

Start at the bottom, and make sure the first louver is level. Use a short, custom-cut board as a spacer so that you can set consistent gaps between boards. With a level bottom louver and accurate spacer, you should be assured of an attractive result.

To install vertical louvers, you can use metal brackets or wood spacers cut from 1×4 lumber. Cut the spacers on a power miter saw for accuracy and efficiency.

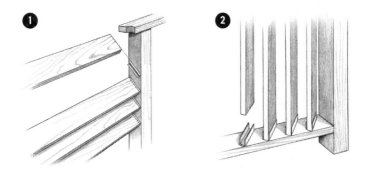

LOUVERS WITH METAL BRACKETS

For horizontal louvers, attach brackets to the posts (1). For vertical louvers, attach brackets to rails that are installed flat between posts (2).

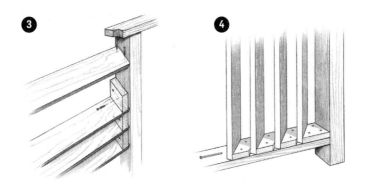

LOUVERS WITH WOOD SPACERS

Wood spacers provide a relatively foolproof means of installing louvers for both horizontal and vertical applications (3). First, cut all of the spacers, then install them one board at a time (4).

Prefab Panels

Preassembled fence panels are a time-saving option, and you can find them in just about any style at home centers and lumberyards. However, before you invest in any prefab fence product, make sure its rails are adequately sized for the weight of the fence and the span between posts, and make sure the fasteners are high quality.

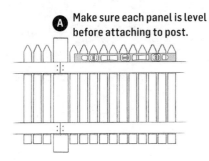

A Make sure each panel is level before attaching to post.

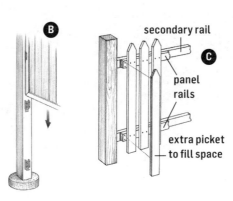

B

C

secondary rail

panel rails

extra picket to fill space

FASTENING PANELS TO POSTS

Prefabricated fence panels are designed with extended rails that can be face nailed to posts (A) or with rails cut flush to the edge of the panel so that the panel can be slid into metal brackets that are installed on the posts (B). If a panel doesn't fit the space you've allocated for it (C), attach secondary rails to the posts and attach the panel rails to those secondary rails. Fill in any empty space with an extra fence board or picket.

Basketweave Fences

Basketweave is another type of board fence that combines texture and pattern with privacy and security. It requires thin boards (⅜" to ½" thick), 4" or 5" wide. These boards are not commonly carried at lumber suppliers, so you may need to special order from a sawmill.

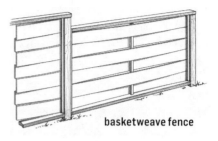

basketweave fence

Attach a 1×2 nailer down the center on the inside faces of each post, and install a vertical 1×3 spacer centered between posts. Place the centers of each board on alternating sides of the spacer, then attach the ends to alternating sides of the nailers using galvanized ring-shank nails.

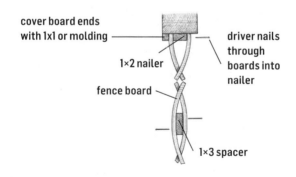

cover board ends with 1x1 or molding

driver nails through boards into nailer

1×2 nailer

fence board

1×3 spacer

LATTICE FENCES

LATTICE FENCES provide a quick and easy method for screening an area. Standard lattice panels are not very strong and are best suited for infill material rather than freestanding structures. Lattice fences are ideal for enclosing and concealing small eyesores, such as garbage cans, or to fill small sections of a fence to break up the monotony of solid-board infill. Using lattice as a fence topper may mean you can exceed the maximum fence height allowed by your local building codes. You can also create a nice privacy screen by installing a 4×6-foot panel of lattice between posts that are spaced 4 feet apart. The open grid of lattice is ideal for support of climbing vines or flowers.

The most commonly available lattice panels are ½" thick, made up of two layers of ¼"-thick slats. A much better choice for fencing is 1"-thick lattice, composed of ½"-thick slats. Lattice can have large or small openings, for providing varying degrees of privacy. While diagonally oriented patterns are most common, lattice with a square orientation often looks better on a finished fence. Vinyl lattice is also readily available in several colors and might be a good choice for a fence topper.

The best way to install lattice panels is to trap them between wood stops that are attached to rails and posts. Install the stops on one side, attach the lattice, and then attach stops on the other side. You may also be able to find channel stock at your lumberyard. Channel stock has a groove already cut into it for holding lattice panels in place.

ATTACHING LATTICE WITH WOOD STOPS

Attach the first 1×1 wood stop to the rail, insert the lattice panel, then attach the second 1×1 wood stop to the rail.

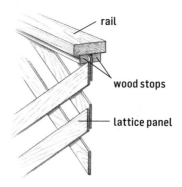

rail

wood stops

lattice panel

ATTACHING LATTICE WITH CHANNEL STOCK

Cut the channel stock to fit the panel (mitering the corners), attach it with glue to the panel, then drive nails or screws through the channel stock and into the posts and rails.

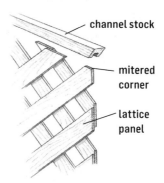

channel stock

mitered corner

lattice panel

CUTTING LATTICE

Lattice can be tricky to cut. I've had the best success using a circular saw while supporting the panel on both sides of the cut line.

1. Set a sheet of plywood across two sawhorses. Place the lattice panel on the plywood. Measure and mark your cut line.

2. Clamp 1×6 boards on top of and underneath the lattice, next to the cut line, so that the lattice is sandwiched in between. Set one or two 1×6 boards beneath the lattice nearby to keep the whole panel level.

3. Set your blade to cut just deep enough to clear the bottom edge of the lattice when your saw is set on the top board, and then make the cut, pushing your saw along the smooth surface of the top board. The boards help keep the lattice from flapping around and separating while you are cutting.

A standard wood blade easily cuts through the staples that hold the slats together, but watch out for sparks — and *always* wear eye protection.

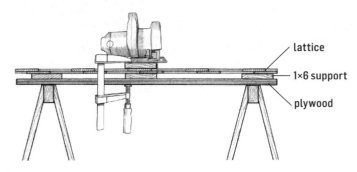

lattice
1×6 support
plywood

VINYL AND OTHER WOOD ALTERNATIVES

POLYVINYL CHLORIDE, or pvc, poly, or vinyl, keeps showing up in an ever-growing number of products in and around our houses: flooring, siding, piping, window frames, and, increasingly, decks and fences. Whether or not vinyl is your cup of tea, in these uses one must admit that it offers strength, ease of installation, long life, low cost, and low maintenance.

Vinyl fences are available in just about any size, shape, or style you can imagine. You will almost certainly pay more initially for vinyl over a similar wood fence, but over the long term you may well save time and money in maintenance and repairs. Vinyl fences do not have to be painted or stained, they will not rot or rust, and they can be effectively washed with a good rainfall. Finally, unlike with wood, you can expect to receive a warranty with your vinyl fence — but be aware that the warranty may require that your fence is professionally installed.

Vinyl fences are sold as complete kits that can include posts, post caps, rails, rail brackets, panel sections, gates, and gate hardware, along with step-by-step instructions. Typically, you set the posts in concrete, allow the concrete to cure, attach brackets to the posts, and then add the rails or panel sections. Post caps and other accessories are normally attached with PVC cement.

Other Wood-Fence Alternatives

An alternative to PVC from within the general family of plastics is high-density polyethylene (HDPE). Fences made with HDPE offer the same benefits as PVC, but they are generally stronger and more durable. The HDPE material performs better in extreme temperatures and stands up well to impact. It is available in a much wider range of colors, including dark colors. I have seen HDPE panels that have a woodlike texture, unlike the smooth, glossy appearance of PVC. And HDPE is nontoxic and easily recyclable.

Composite fencing is yet another alternative to wood. Composite fencing material is made with a combination of wood particles and (largely) recycled plastic, the same material used in the popular decking material. Composites offer the same low-maintenance and durability benefits as vinyl fencing but are made from a more environmentally friendly material. Style and installation options vary by manufacturer and product line.

Rustic Fences

A rustic fence may be inspired by age-old techniques and materials, utilizing few tools and little if any hardware. These fences are often permitted to show their wrinkles through natural aging and weathering. Often made low with natural, unmilled wood, rustic fences make great garden borders and ornamental landscape features.

RUSTIC-LOOKING POSTS AND RAILS are available at home and garden centers. This style features tapered rails that fit through mortises and are held in place by nails driven through the posts.

A "FOUND WOOD" FENCE can be made from longer wood pieces to resemble a post-and-rail fence. In this case, however, the posts do not necessarily have to be buried, and the rails and posts can be tied together with twine or wire.

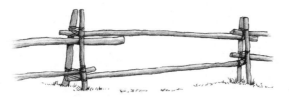

WATTLE FENCES are built with a combination of weaving and construction. With posts buried in the ground a few feet apart, green saplings are woven through the posts in a pattern of your choosing.

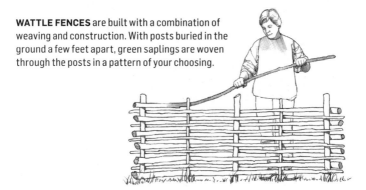

CHOOSING AND APPLYING A FINISH

EXTERIOR WOOD FINISHES fall into two basic categories: film-forming and penetrating. Penetrating finishes soak into the wood to provide deep protection, while film-forming finishes create a protective barrier on the wood's surface. Either type of finish can be used on a fence, with different visual effects and different levels of protection and longevity.

Penetrating Finishes

Penetrating finishes allow the wood to breathe and the wood grain to show through. Since they sink into the wood rather than forming a surface film, they do not peel or chip as they age.

Clear penetrating finishes protect wood while retaining the wood's natural color. Basic clear wood finishes provide protection against water damage only and will not prevent fading from sun exposure. They are the least durable choices and need to be reapplied every year or 2. Water-repellent preservatives containing mildewcide, ultraviolet (UV) stabilizers, and other decay-fighting ingredients provide extra protection.

Semitransparent stains contain pigments that help the finish provide significantly more protection against sun damage than clear finishes, including those with UV stabilizers. An oil-based semitransparent stain with a mildewcide is the best choice for a fence (unless you want to paint). Semitransparent stains typically need to be renewed every 2 to 5 years.

Film-Forming Finishes

Both paints and solid-color (opaque) stains are film-forming finishes that seal wood with a protective layer on its surface. Solid-color stains contain more pigment than semitransparent stains but less than paint. Lacquer, urethane, and shellac are also film-forming finishes, but they should not be used on outdoor structures.

Because it does not allow the wood to breathe, the surface of a film-forming finish is prone to cracking and peeling, which can be an eyesore, particularly with paint. When it's time to recoat, stained wood generally does not require as much preparation as paint: the surface needs to be cleaned, but usually not scraped or stripped, as with paint. Solid-color stains can last about 3 to 6 years before needing a recoat.

For longevity, nothing beats a careful paint job, which should be good for 5 to 8 years. It's best to start with a coat of paintable water-repellent preservative, followed by a coat of stain-blocking latex primer, and then two coats of 100 percent acrylic latex paint. I like to apply the preservative and let it dry in warm, sunny weather for a couple of days, and then add a stain-blocking latex primer and the first coat of paint before I even assemble the fence. Using this method, every surface is protected. The second coat of paint can be applied after the fence is completed. *Note:* Read the labels carefully when shopping for a water-repellent preservative, as most of these products are not suitable for painting.

Tips for Applying Finishes

- Finish standard, dry lumber as soon as possible. Waiting is advisable only if the wood is "green" (unseasoned) or if it received factory-applied water repellent.

- Use a brush for the first — and most important — coat. You can follow with a paint sprayer, roller, or pump sprayer on some fences, but sprayers waste too much paint on fences with spaced boards. Follow spraying with a brush to ensure complete coverage.

- To remove any surface glaze that can inhibit absorption, sand smooth-planed lumber lightly before applying the first coat. Rough-sawn lumber does not need sanding.

- Apply a penetrating finish as directed. With solid-color stains, prime the wood first, then apply two coats of stain. Avoid permanent lap marks (dark splotches created when wet stain is applied over dried stain) by working in the shade and applying finish on small sections at a time.

- Hide knots in painted finishes by applying a stain-blocking primer designed to stop bleed-through from wood tannins.

CHAPTER THREE

METAL FENCES

Metal is adaptable to almost any fencing need, from high-end residential to remote, rural applications. Most types of metal fence can be constructed quickly and require little upkeep and maintenance. This chapter focuses on the two most common types of metal fencing: ornamental metal (the modern answer to traditional wrought iron) and chain link. If all you need is an effective barrier to corral pets or keep critters out of your garden, a simple mesh fence should do the trick.

ORNAMENTAL METAL FENCES

IT IS HARD TO THINK OF any fencing material that offers a better combination of security, beauty, strength, durability, and see-through visibility than wrought iron. But building an authentic wrought-iron fence requires a great deal of labor. Each piece of iron must be heated and shaped or twisted, then joined to the main structure. Cast iron has largely replaced wrought iron for fencing because single molds can be used to create endless quantities of identical metal pieces.

Most of what passes for wrought iron these days is really a much lighter and less expensive imitation that is made out of aluminum, steel, or (the new, nonmetallic kid on the block) composite or polymer materials. All of these are available in styles that mimic traditional wrought iron, at least from a distance. Many contemporary styles are also available. Ornamental metal fences are sold in kits that can be easily transported and assembled by do-it-yourselfers.

Choosing Modern Ornamental Fencing

DIY-friendly ornamental fencing is sold in kit form, and it's a good idea to buy all of the materials from the same manufacturer. Each product has its own style and methods of assembly. Welded steel tends to be somewhat stronger than aluminum, but the latter offers the great advantage of being rust-resistant and, therefore, requires less long-term maintenance. Steel fence sections often are welded on site by contractors. Alternatively, steel fencing can be purchased in preassembled sections, which the do-it-yourselfer can complete on-site. Aluminum fencing is more likely to be put together with screws, nuts, and brackets.

Black is the traditional standard for most metal fencing, but color options are improving all the time. You can find powder-coated steel and aluminum ornamental fencing in a range of lighter colors, which is a popular option for pool enclosures.

Most manufacturers offer several options of strength and security with metal fence gates. Popular upgrades include self-closing and self-latching gates with keyed deadbolts — all included in a package and easy to install.

KIT ASSEMBLY

Ornamental fence kits typically use bolts and screws to attach rails to posts, but the exact mechanism can differ from manufacturer to manufacturer.

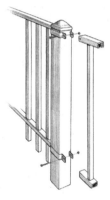

inset bracket
attachments

"mortised" posts with
"tenon" rails

decorative
wraparound bracket
attachments

Nonmetal "Metal" Fencing

Ornamental metal has several "faux" versions. Some iterations are manufactured from a mixture of polypropylene and fiberglass, while others are all fiberglass and are made through a process called pultrusion. Pultruded fiberglass is commonly used for making high-strength floor grates for industrial and commercial applications. Polypropylene is the primary material used to make composite decking boards (and fencing). Manufacturers claim that nonmetal fencing is fade resistant, durable, and virtually maintenance-free. Regardless of these claims, a fence made from this material will not rust and will never need to be painted or stained.

One composite system I've seen comes in 6-foot-long sections at 4 to 5 feet in height. The sections are joined by concealed fasteners, which is a nice improvement over aluminum fences. The gates are steel-reinforced and feature self-closing hinges and latches.

1. Establish the fence line with string stretching from corner to corner.

2. Measure and mark the posthole locations.

3. Bury posts in holes at least 30" deep, centered every 6 feet.

4. After setting the first post, immediately assemble one fence section and slide it into the post.

5. Set the next post in its hole, attach it to the section, and pour concrete into the hole. Regularly check the posts for plumb and the rails for level, then secure the top rail to the posts with screws driven through the insides of the hollow posts.

6. Attach post caps and, if desired, finial caps on the pickets.

CHAIN-LINK FENCES

FIRST PRODUCED IN EUROPE in the 1850s, chain link became a fixture of the American landscape through the twentieth century. It offers a great combination of security with visibility, and is strong, long-lasting, and affordable. It stands up well to regular use and is relatively easy to install.

Standard galvanized chain link will not win any beauty contests (and therefore is not the best choice for front yards), but a few options can make the material more attractive. Color-coated chain link — in green, brown, or black — can blend in nicely with many environments. Colored chain-link fencing with square posts has a nicer look than the same fence with

ANATOMY OF A CHAIN-LINK FENCE

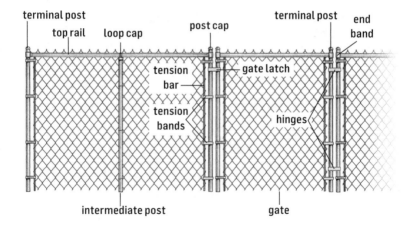

standard round posts, if for no other reason than because it is different. Weaving colored slats through the chain-link mesh is another way to improve the look. Slats are available in a wide range of colors and often are used to add privacy. Alternatively, tall plants or vines that climb up and through the mesh can help to obscure the fence.

Chain link comes in heights of 3 feet to 12 feet. The most common height is 4 feet, which is an easy height for do-it-your-selfers to install. Taller fences can be tricky to install and probably should be left to fencing contractors.

Shopping for Parts

There are many manufacturers of chain link, and although the parts are often interchangeable, I think it's best to buy everything you need from one supplier. There are quality differences, so it pays to shop around and ask some questions. After deciding on height and surface coating, the key factors to consider are gauge and mesh size. The size of the framework (posts and rails) is typically informed by the height and intended use of the fence.

Gauge is a standard measurement of the diameter of wire: the higher the number, the thinner (and weaker) the metal. You can find chain link in gauges ranging from 6 to 14, but for most residential purposes I would suggest something in the range of 9 to 11½. Wire that is thinner than 11½ gauge stands a much better chance of being damaged over time.

Mesh size. The size of the mesh relates to both visibility and strength. Smaller mesh means that more wire must be used in the fence, which adds to its strength (while reducing visibility).

Mesh under 1" is generally found only in high-security installations. Swimming pools and tennis courts are often enclosed with 1¼" to 1¾" mesh, while standard yard fences rely on mesh of 2" or more. Obviously, thicker-gauge metal and smaller mesh size will translate into greater expense, so you'll want to choose carefully. One other factor to keep in mind is that kids have a strong preference for bigger mesh, which allows ample room for their toes. This is to say, the bigger the mesh, the easier the fence is to climb.

Framework. The chain-link mesh material itself (often called "fabric" in the trade) is not the only component that affects strength and durability of a finished fence. The posts and rails that constitute the fence frame are also critical to the lasting quality of a chain-link fence. Posts and rails are offered in different strengths and sizes. Manufacturers tend to break down the choices into categories based on the height of the fence and the degree of use it will get (light, medium, or heavy). Terminal posts (those used at ends, corners, and gate openings) are the largest, followed in size by the intermediate posts and then the top rail. Sleeve connectors are used to join sections of top rail.

Fittings. The fabric is joined to the frame with a variety of fittings, including bands, rings, nuts, bolts, and gate hinges and latches. The completed fence is only as strong as these fittings, so you should carefully compare the hardware that accompanies different product lines. Make sure that any warranty that comes with the fencing covers all components.

INSTALLING CHAIN LINK

The installation of a chain-link fence is pretty straightforward. Your fencing may or may not come with detailed instructions. The following guidelines should help you through a typical installation. However, this guidance should not be treated as a substitute for any instructions from the manufacturer.

SETTING THE POSTS

1. The first tasks for installing a chain-link fence are similar to those for a wood fence (see chapter 2). Begin by setting up string lines, making sure all corners are square. Use stakes to mark locations for all terminal posts, and then add stakes for the intermediate posts. The fence manufacturer should specify the post spacing, but you can reduce this maximum spacing a bit to ensure that the posts are evenly spaced. Do not, however, follow this policy with gateposts, which must be spaced exactly as directed.

2. Dig 8"-diameter holes for the terminal posts and 6"-diameter holes for intermediate posts. In cold climates, dig all holes below the frost line. In climates where frost is not a concern, terminal posts should be set in 30"-deep holes and intermediate posts in 24"-deep holes. Brace the terminal posts so that they are centered in their holes and are plumb. Use clamps or duct tape to hold the braces to the posts. It's standard to set terminal posts 2" higher than the height of the fencing material, but confirm this with your manufacturer instructions.

3. Carefully fill the holes with concrete. Use a margin trowel to smooth the concrete and slope it slightly away from the posts. Let the concrete cure for two days before disturbing the posts. After the concrete has hardened, tie a string line between the posts exactly 4" down from the top. The string line must be taut and should be centered on the posts, not aligned with one side or the other. Set the intermediate posts in their holes in concrete, centered with and at the height of the string line.

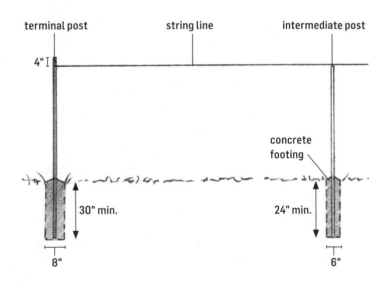

terminal post string line intermediate post

4" I

concrete footing

30" min. 24" min.

8" 6"

ATTACHING FASTENERS AND RAILS

1. Allow the concrete around the intermediate posts to cure for two days, and then begin attaching the fittings to the terminal posts. Typically, you will need three tension bands on each post for fencing up to 5 feet high (add one tension band for each additional foot of height), along with one rail-end fitting and a post cap. Corner posts require double the number of tension bands and rail-end fittings because these posts serve fencing that is heading in two different directions. These bands slip easily over the posts and are secured with bolts and nuts.

2. Set loop caps on all of the intermediate posts, and then slide the rail through them and into the rail-end fittings. If necessary, cut the rails with a hacksaw and use sleeve connectors to combine two rail sections. *Note:* Some types

Working with Slopes

On a gradual slope, you can set all the posts at the same height above ground so the fencing follows the slope perfectly, as in Sloped framing (page 24). More pronounced slopes may require a terraced pattern similar to Stepped framing (page 22). For more complex sites, consult your supplier or the manufacturer for recommendations.

of rail are made with smaller diameters on one end. This design allows them to slip into another rail, and therefore requires no connectors.

TERMINAL POST FITTING

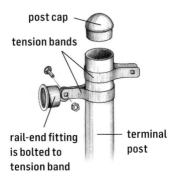

post cap

tension bands

rail-end fitting is bolted to tension band

terminal post

INTERMEDIATE POST FITTING

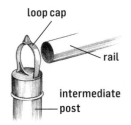

loop cap

rail

intermediate post

SLEEVE CONNECTOR

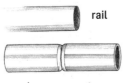

rail

sleeve connector

ADDING THE FENCING

This step is easier to accomplish with a helper who holds up the fencing while you make the connections.

1. Unroll the fencing along the fence line, stretching it from one terminal post to the next. Slide a tension bar through the mesh on one end, and then fasten the tension bar to the tension bands with bolts and nuts. Tighten the nuts with a socket wrench while holding the bolt head steady with an adjustable wrench.

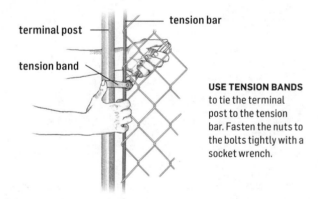

terminal post

tension bar

tension band

USE TENSION BANDS to tie the terminal post to the tension bar. Fasten the nuts to the bolts tightly with a socket wrench.

2. The key to a strong, secure chain-link fence is to stretch the fencing tightly to minimize slack. Your supplier should be able to rent, sell, or lend you a special pulling bar or stretcher to simplify this work. You can do a satisfactory job with the pulling bar alone, but it's best

to use it with a come-along. Attach the pulling bar to the fencing, or to a stretcher or tension bar inserted into the fencing temporarily. Hook one end of the come-along to the pulling bar and the other to the next terminal post. Slowly tighten the fencing until it is taut, then insert a tension bar and attach the fencing to the tension bands on the terminal posts.

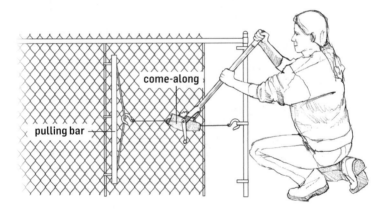

WITH THE FENCING ATTACHED TO ONE TERMINAL POST, use a pulling bar or stretcher and a come-along to pull the slack out of the fencing before fastening it to the other terminal post.

3. If the fencing is too long, use pliers to open a loop at the top and bottom of the wire mesh at the spot you want it to separate. Unweave one of the wires through the links until the fence comes apart. To join two sections of fencing, first remove a strand of wire from the end of one section, and then use that wire to tie the two pieces together.

REMOVE EXCESS FENCING by loosening the loops of the same wire at the top and bottom of the fence and then unwinding the wire.

4. With the fencing attached to the terminal posts, use tie wire every 12" to secure the mesh to the rails and posts. Some suppliers offer special S-shaped ties to simplify this task. Repeat this process for each section of fencing.

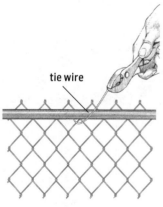

tie wire

USING PLIERS, ATTACH THE FENCING to the top rails and intermediate posts with tie wire.

INSTALLING THE GATE

Most chain-link fences have matching gates (again, buy the
gates from the same supplier/manufacturer as the fencing).
Adding a gate is all about attaching hardware. First decide
which way you want the gate to swing, then attach the two
gatepost hinges to the appropriate gatepost, about 8" from the
top and bottom (a tall gate may require more hinges). The
pins on the hinges should point toward each other, as shown
in the accompanying illustration. Next, attach the gate frame
hinges to the gate frame, and then hang the gate in place.
With the bottom of the gate about 2" above ground, tighten
all the nuts and bolts on the hinges. Finally, fasten the latch
to the other side of the gate at a comfortable height.

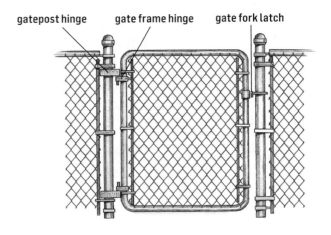

gatepost hinge   gate frame hinge   gate fork latch

MESH FENCING

METAL MESH IS FENCING STRIPPED down to its most elementary, functional essence. Determine exactly what you want the fencing to keep in or out, then choose the appropriate fence construction and mesh material.

Choosing Mesh

Mesh fencing can be knotted, welded, or woven, depending on the function of the fence and the gauge of the metal used. Welded and woven fencing is most common, but knotted mesh offers flexibility that's appropriate for rolling terrain (some types of knotted mesh have sharp edges and so aren't suitable for animals or kids).

The gauge, or thickness, of mesh wire ranges from very thin 20- or 24-gauge wire used on netting to thick 9- or 10-gauge wire used for heavy-animal enclosures. The size of the mesh openings ranges from ¼" squares to 2" x 4" rectangles or diamonds. Fencing height starts at 12" and goes up to 72". Terminology may vary by manufacturer or supplier, but here are the basic types:

Hardware cloth. Thin (19- to 23-gauge) wire produced with small mesh sizes (¼" or ½" square). For light-duty fencing, such as for small rabbit cages.

Poultry netting. Typically 20- or 22-gauge wire woven into hexagonal shapes. Mesh sizes range from ⅝" to 2". Lightweight and easy to handle; often used for low-cost garden fencing.

Small-animal fencing. Often used to keep rabbits and rodents out of gardens. Mesh openings at the bottom of the fence are smaller than those at the top. Heights range from 28" to 40".

Apron fencing. Includes a preformed apron on the bottom, which is laid horizontally a few inches below ground to prevent animals from burrowing under the fence. You can provide similar protection with standard fencing by bending and burying a portion of the bottom edge of the mesh.

General-purpose mesh fencing. Also called *utility, garden,* or *kennel fencing,* this type is typically welded wire fencing with uniform, rectangular mesh. Used for garden and small-animal enclosures. Mesh sizes include ½" × 1" to 2" × 4", in heights up to 72". Heavy-duty 2" mesh makes a less expensive but suitable alternative to chain link. Green vinyl-coated 3" × 2" mesh is popular for garden enclosures.

Fence Construction

To build a permanent mesh fence, use 4×4 wood posts set in the footing of your choice (see chapter 2). Attach the mesh to the posts with galvanized fence staples (U-shaped nails). For a temporary or seasonal barrier, metal T-posts go in quickly and stay put without a footing. Attach mesh to metal posts with wire or wire clips designed for this purpose, or use posts with small hooks that you cinch over the mesh wires with a hammer.

CHAPTER FOUR

GATES

Gates are the "business end" of the fence, the doorway that makes the fence a functional item. While fences are pretty simple structures, gates can be fairly complex. To endure the everyday rigors of opening and closing (not to mention the constant pull of gravity) gates must be, above all else, well built. But don't sweat it; if you can build even a small fence, you'll have no trouble building the gate (and you'll probably enjoy it a lot more than the fence building).

DESIGN DECISIONS

GATES ARE USUALLY MADE FROM metal or wood, but when making your own, you are pretty much restricted to the latter. With ornamental metal fences, gates can be purchased along with the fence and should be installed as directed by the manufacturer.

Wood gates can be used with just about any type of fence. The big question is *what style of gate to build.* With front-yard wood fences, I like gates that closely resemble the fence but have a feature or two that make them stand out. This can be done by using the same wood and finish as the fence itself while adding a subtle change or two. Perhaps the gate sits a bit higher or lower than the fence, or is placed between two visually prominent posts.

Distinctive features make a gate easy to identify and thus more welcoming to visitors. On the other hand, if a welcoming entry is what you want to avoid (say, for privacy or security reasons), then your goal should be to match the gate exactly to the fence so they appear to constitute a seamless barrier. A seamless look can also complement certain house styles.

How Wide?

You can build a gate about as wide or as narrow as you want. But, being of a practical mind, I suggest that you plan to make it 4 feet wide, and then determine if there is any good reason to adjust that plan.

Begin by considering what will need to get through the gate, such as garden carts and lawn tractors, in addition to people and pets. At 4 feet, a gate will most likely be wider than the exterior doors on your house, which should mean that it could accommodate anything currently in the home.

One advantage of keeping the opening at or less than 4 feet is that a single gate can handle the span between the posts. With larger sizes you might need to consider a double gate. For particularly large, heavy gates, such as those serving driveways, it's advisable to hire a professional rather than tackle the project yourself.

Location and Swing

An existing sidewalk, driveway, or pathway normally dictates where the gate goes. But if you're relandscaping you might choose an alternative location. For example, if you're redoing an entry sidewalk, you might consider offsetting the gate from the house entry, so the path between the gate and house door is curved. This design can add privacy if you plant shrubs along the sidewalk.

Another design trick is to set the gate in from the fence a few feet. This inset not only calls additional attention to the entry, even if the gate is designed to look like the rest of the fence, but it also positions the entry out of the flow of traffic, which can be a real blessing if the fence is set along a well-traveled road, path, or sidewalk.

When it comes to how the gate swings, decide whether it should swing out, in, or both ways — and whether it should be hinged on the right side or left side. Most front-yard gates swing in toward the house (rather than out into sidewalk traffic). Gates on backyard fences can swing either way but may be restricted by sloping ground or other natural obstructions, such as trees. In any case, always confirm the gate can open easily in the desired direction.

Gateposts

As discussed in chapter 2, gateposts are different from all other fence posts: They not only help support the fence but also the gate, which is routinely swinging back and forth and is frequently knocked around by people and objects passing through. The post that holds the gate hinges is under the greatest strain, but both gateposts need to be treated with more care than other posts. Ideally, gateposts should be heavier than the other posts and be buried deeper and backfilled more securely. They also must be perfectly plumb to ensure proper gate operation.

Regardless of what style of backfill you use on other posts or the depth at which you bury them, gateposts should be placed 6" to 12" below the frost line and be set in concrete. If frost is not an issue where you live, set the posts at least 30" deep.

In terms of size, use 4×4 posts for gates up to 3 feet wide, 6×6s for gates 3 to 5 feet wide, and 8×8s for anything larger than that. These dimensions can be a bit flexible, depending on the weight of the gate and the amount of use it will receive, but you'll never regret using bigger posts.

Gate Frame Options

There are two basic styles of wood gate frames. A full perimeter frame is usually the strongest and can be adapted to most fence styles. A Z-frame is relatively simple and has light appearance, but due to their lower strength I don't recommend Z-frames for gates wider than 3 feet. If you'd like to have both strength and a thin profile, build a perimeter frame with the 2×4s set flat rather than on edge, using half-lap joints at the corner (see page 106).

Gate frames are sometimes built with 1×4s or 1×6s, but I would use such thin boards only if the gate is very light and small and the thin boards are vital to the gate's appearance. A compromise between 1× and 2× lumber is $\frac{5}{4}$ (called five-quarter) wood, which measures about 1" thick.

GATE FRAME OPTIONS

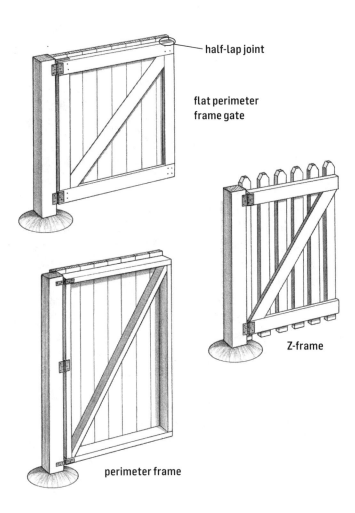

half-lap joint

flat perimeter
frame gate

Z-frame

perimeter frame

MAKING HALF-LAP JOINTS

When using a circular saw, clamp the 2×4, flat side down, to a sawhorse or other sturdy work surface. This allows you to keep both hands on the saw for clean, consistent cuts. If you have a table saw but no dado blade, you can use this same approach.

1. Mark the board 3½" from its end. Set the saw blade to cut exactly one-half the measured thickness of the board. Make a series of closely spaced cuts until you reach the mark.

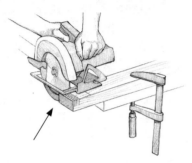

2. Use a hammer to knock out the thin pieces of wood, then use a chisel and clean out the notched area. Repeat for the other board. Test-fit the joint and adjust the notches if necessary. Attach the boards at the laps with glue and 1¼" screws.

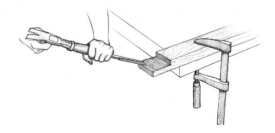

GATE BRACING

Diagonal bracing is a critical element of the frame, but it is frequently misunderstood and/or misapplied. A properly positioned wood brace transfers forces, or loads, from the top edge of the latch side of the gate down toward the bottom hinge, which is the strongest corner of the gate. If a wood brace is angled in the reverse direction, it actually encourages the gate to sag. (The hinge side is tied directly to a post and so does not sag, but the latch side is suspended and therefore is subject to gravity and other downward forces, including kids who like taking a ride on the gate.) For the load to be directed efficiently, the wood bracing must be installed tight against the horizontal boards of the gate.

DIAGONAL BRACING WITH CABLE

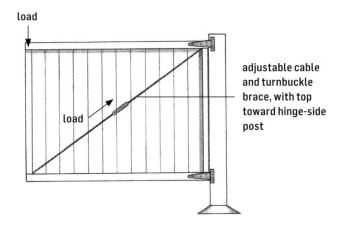

load

load

adjustable cable and turnbuckle brace, with top toward hinge-side post

DIAGONAL BRACING WITH WOOD

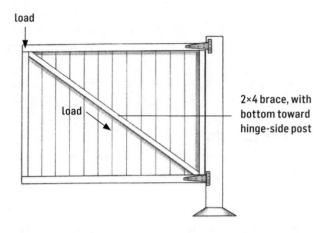

load

load

2×4 brace, with
bottom toward
hinge-side post

By contrast, when bracing a gate with a cable (tensioned with a turnbuckle), the cable runs from the bottom corner on the latch side up toward the top corner on the hinge side.

Hence, a wood brace relies on compression, or crushing force; a cable works under tension, or pulling force.

GATE HARDWARE

SELECT YOUR HARDWARE BEFORE you build your fence. Learn how it installs and how much space on the side of the gate it needs to function properly, and then finalize the dimensions and style of your gate.

You can usually find a pretty good selection of hardware at one of the large home improvement stores. Smaller lumberyards and hardware stores often have a limited selection but are able to make special orders through catalogs. Two major manufacturers are Stanley Hardware and National Hardware, and both have websites that display their full product lines (see Resources, page 120).

Gate hardware tends to be either ornamental or utilitarian. Ornamental hardware is usually black and formed into attractive shapes. Utilitarian hardware has a dull galvanized or shiny zinc-plated finish and is not really intended to be admired for its looks. The price difference between these styles often is less than you might think.

Hinges

Select hinges based on function, look, installation, price . . . and whatever other criteria you deem important. But always go for quality hinges that are big enough and strong enough for the job at hand. Here's a look at the basic types:

T-hinges. The most basic style of gate hinge. They usually have a nonremovable pin with a vertically oriented "mounting leaf" (the side that attaches to the post) and a horizontally oriented "door leaf" (the side that attaches to the gate).

T-hinges

Strap hinges. Long, identical leaves on each side of the pivoting pin. They are most common on large gates and often have removable pins.

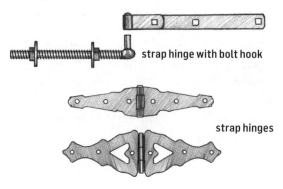

strap hinge with bolt hook

strap hinges

Spring hinges. These make the gate self-closing. Choose hinges with adjustable tension, as too much tension creates a nuisance and can be dangerous for kids and less-able adults. An alternative is a hydraulic closer (Kant-Slam is one brand), which is self-closing and highly adjustable. You need only one hydraulic closer per gate, along with one or two regular hinges.

Screw and bolt hinges. These include a strap leaf that attaches to the gate and a lag-screw-style screw hook or through-bolt hook that anchors to the gatepost. They can handle heavy gates and can be installed for either swing direction. Screw hooks are handy for round gateposts, while bolted versions are easy to tighten during periodic maintenance.

Latches

The most important criteria for choosing a gate latch are security, ease of use, and appearance. Ease of installation may also be a factor, and the size or style of your gate may limit your choices somewhat. With short gates, you can mount a latch on the inside that can be easily reached from the outside. But for taller gates, you'll need a latch that can be operated from both sides.

Slide-action bolt. Offers modest strength and some security; can be secured with a padlock.

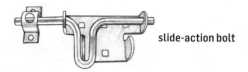

slide-action bolt

Hasp latch. Can be locked with a padlock and offers security when the latch is highly visible or accessible. Those with hasps that cover the mounting screws are most secure.

Automatic gate latch. Combines both latch and stop. Some can be secured with a padlock, and most have a lever that allows the latch to be operated from the opposite side of the gate by a pullcord, which you need to install.

automatic latch

Thumb latch. Classic decorative gate latch that can be operated from both sides. Check the thickness of the gate before purchasing; many thumb latches don't work on gates thicker than 2⅝".

Cane bolt. This secures the gate with a steel shaft that drops down into a hole in the ground. This is commonly used to secure one or both doors of a double-door gate. Cane bolts can also hold gates open via a second hole.

Gotta Stop It

Automatic latches stop the gate from swinging too far. If you use another type of latch you might need to add a custom stop to halt the gate in its closed position. A gate stop can be as simple as a strip of wood installed on the latch-side gatepost (much like stop molding on a standard door). You can also build the gate (or the fence) so that the last infill board overhangs the framing a bit to serve as a stop.

BUILDING THE GATE

It's a good idea to work out the details and dimensions of your gate on paper before you begin construction. You can prepare a scaled drawing, but it's even better to draw a full-scale replica of the gate on a sheet of plywood, and then use the drawing as a working template. This is particularly helpful with a Z-frame gate, because you can set the face of the gate down on the template with the boards aligned and spaced properly before you attach the three framing boards. With a perimeter frame, it's usually easier to construct the frame first, and then attach the infill to it.

MEASURE THE OPENING

1. Measure between gateposts at the top and bottom of the opening. If the distances are the same, the gateposts are plumb (nice job). If not, take a little time to square the opening. You can accomplish this either by repositioning, shaving a little wood from, or adding shims to one or both posts.

2. Next, calculate the width of the gate by subtracting ½" for clearance on the latch side and ¼" on the hinge side. This ¾" overall clearance is a standard dimension for gates with normal T-hinges and standard latches. You may need to increase the clearance for other types of hardware or unusually thick gates.

ASSEMBLE THE FRAME

1. Cut the top and bottom frame members to the exact dimension of the gate's width, then cut the two vertical side boards to fit in between. The length of these vertical sides depends on your design. You may want to make them short enough to allow infill boards to overlap at the bottom and, especially, at the top.

2. If you're building a perimeter frame with flat boards, cut and join the half-lap joints. For an on-edge frame, lay out the four boards, and use a framing square to make sure all four corners are square. If you don't have a framing square, measure the diagonals from the outside corners; the frame is square when the diagonal dimensions are equal.

3. Clamp the pieces (if you have long enough clamps). Fasten them with screws or nails through the top and bottom boards and into the ends of the side boards. For a large, heavy gate, lag screws provide a stronger connection than other fastener types. With either type of frame, lay the uncut brace on the work surface, set the frame on top, and confirm that the frame is square. Use the frame to mark the cut lines of the brace, then cut the brace to length and attach it to the frame.

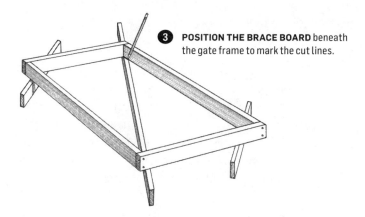

3 **POSITION THE BRACE BOARD** beneath the gate frame to mark the cut lines.

ATTACH THE INFILL

1. Set the frame flat on the work surface with the hinge side of the brace nearest to you. If you are using the same type of infill on the gate as the fence, use the same fasteners for the fence and the gate. If your fence has spaced vertical boards or pickets, maintain consistent spacing between the boards from fence to gate to achieve a clean look.

2. It's a good idea to set the infill in place loosely to check the fit before fastening. If necessary, trim small amounts off several boards so that any deviation in spacing is hard to notice. To cut a pattern on the top or bottom ends of the infill boards, install the boards a bit long, and then trim them to length later. Set the gate in place and check the fit.

HANG THE GATE

1. Mount the hinges to the gate before installing the gate. Always fasten hinges to the gate framing, not just to the infill boards. Two hinges are sufficient for most gates up to 4 feet tall; three are recommended for 6-footers. Use screws long enough to penetrate at least 2" into the frame. For large strap hinges on a heavy gate, use carriage bolts with washers and nuts instead of screws.

2. Set the gate in the opening, resting it on wood blocks or bricks so it's at the exact installation height, and make sure it's level. *Tip:* After leveling, slip a small shim under the latch end; once the gate hangs freely, gravity will usually bring the latch side down a bit and bring the gate into proper alignment.

3. Drive a single screw into each hinge. Let the gate hang freely while you check the alignment and swing. Adjust as needed, and then install the remaining screws. Install a gate stop, if necessary (see Gotta Stop It, page 114).

4. Install the latch last. Because new gates tend to settle, you can wait a few days or even weeks before installing the latch. However, if you're using an automatic latch (which also serves as a stop), you should clamp or fasten a temporary stop to the latch side of the gatepost, in the meantime, to prevent the gate from swinging too far when closed. After the gate has settled, simply remove the temporary stop and install the automatic latch.

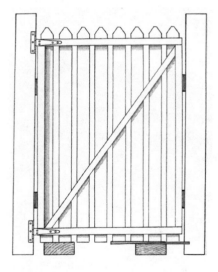

PROP THE GATE IN THE OPENING so that it is level. Then slip a shim under the bottom on the latch side. Attach the hinges with the gate set in this slightly tapered position. Once the props are removed and gravity takes over, the gate will settle into proper alignment.

RESOURCES

Ameristar Fence Products
888-333-3422
www.ameristarfence.com

California Redwood Association
925-935-1499
www.calredwood.org

Great Fence
888-379-1312
www.greatfence.com

Hoover Fence Co.
800-355-2335
www.hooverfence.com

National Hardware
www.natman.com

Online Fence Supply
980-355-2749
www.onlinefencesupply.com

Pool Safely
U.S. Consumer Product Safety
Commission
301-504-7900
www.poolsafely.gov
Pool and spa safety guidelines

Stanley Hardware
www.stanleyhardware.com

INDEX

Page numbers in *italic* indicate illustrations.

OTHER STOREY TITLES YOU WILL ENJOY

The Fence Bible by Jeff Beneke
A complete resource for building fences that enhance the landscape while fulfilling basic functions.
272 pages. Paper. ISBN 978-1-58017-530-2.

Fences for Pasture & Garden by Gail Damerow
Sound, up-to-date advice and instruction to make building fences a task anyone can tackle with confidence.
160 pages. Paper. ISBN 978-0-88266-753-9.

Five-Plant Gardens by Nancy J. Ondra
Illustrated garden plans and season-by-season growing highlights for 52 perennial gardens, each one featuring just five plants.
184 pages. Paper. ISBN 978-1-61212-004-1.

The Vegetable Gardner's Book of Building Projects by the Editors of Storey Publishing
Simple-to-make projects, including cold frames, compost bins, planters, raised beds, outdoor furniture, and more.
152 pages. Paper. ISBN 978-1-60342-526-1.

Woodworking FAQ by Spike Carlsen
Practical answers to common woodworking questions, plus insider tips on how to be successful in every project.
304 pages. Paper with partially concealed wire-o.
ISBN 978-1-60342-729-6.

These and other books from Storey Publishing are available wherever quality books are sold or by calling 1-800-441-5700.
Visit us at *www.storey.com* or sign up for our newsletter at *www.storey.com/signup*.